SAMSON CARRYING THE GATES OF GAZA.

# THE GIANT JUDGE

OR THE

# STORY OF SAMSON.

BY REV. W. A. SCOTT, D. D.,
OF SAN FRANCISCO.

——"There will I build him
A monument,——
With all his trophies hung, and acts enrolled
In copious legend, or sweet lyric song.
Thither shall all the valiant youth resort,
And from his memory inflame their breasts
To matchless valour, and adventures high:
The virgins also shall, on feastful days,
Visit his tomb with flowers."—*Samson Agonistes.*

PHILADELPHIA:
PRESBYTERIAN BOARD OF PUBLICATION.
NO. 821 CHESTNUT STREET.

STEREOTYPED BY JESPER HARDING & SON,
INQUIRER BUILDING, SOUTH THIRD STREET, PHILA.

# CONTENTS.

# INTRODUCTION.

In this little volume I have a definite end in view. I candidly acknowledge that, with me, the reality of Bible histories is an indispensable condition to faith in the doctrines and precepts of Christianity. It is my purpose therefore, so far as the subject seems to come properly within the reach of these pages, to consider the history of Samson as a *true history*, explain its meaning, and apply its principles. Unless biblical memoirs are strictly true—a record of things as they were, and of facts as they did occur—if the men named are nations or myths, and not individuals—if the miracles wrought by Moses and Samson are mere natural phenomena or figures of speech; then I have no confidence that the doctrines of the Bible are from God.

I am well aware that some do not like the subject I have chosen—they would prefer Joseph or Daniel as a hero. Others are ready to pronounce the effort as useless—and some consider it as "an idle attempt to collect evidence," on a subject that does not admit of proof; and others will charge me with maintaining most uncritical, ignorant, unphilosophical, baseless assumptions in regard to the histories of the Bible, and the literal interpretation of the scriptures. But as *Keil* in his preface to Joshua expresses it, I am persuaded that "The great want of the Church, at the present day, is a clear comprehension of the meaning of the Old Testament, in its fulness and purity, in order that the God of Israel may again be universally recognized as the eternal God, whose faithfulness is unchangeable, the one living and true God, who performed all that he did to Israel for our instruction and salvation, having chosen Abraham and his seed to be his people, to preserve his revelations, that from him the whole world might receive salvation, and in him all the families of the earth be blessed."

The great Augustine in his one hundred and sixtieth sermon is correct in saying most emphatically, Novum Testamentum in vetere velabatur: Vetus Testamentum in novo revelatur. "The New Testament was veiled in the Old; the Old Testament is revealed in the New." If the gospel of Jesus Christ is therefore the only way of salvation, the historical reality of the Old Testament must be fully established. It is true, that the good things of which in the old economy we have only the *shadows*, have come in all their precious realities: but it does not follow that the old economy is wholly obsolete. When a fond mother folds in her arms a living son returned from distant lands, or with honour from many a bloody field of battle, she does not indeed in the moment of transport turn from the living face to gaze on the cold picture. The artist may not choose to study his subject in twilight, when he may have it in the full blaze of day. And yet, that fond mother may by the help of the portrait discover some line of beauty in her son's face, which she had not observed without it: and the artist may find that some sharp and simple outlines of the mountain or of the palace ruins are brought much more impressively before his eye against a twilight sky than in the glare of day. The great truths of Christianity stand up boldly in the history of God's ancient people, just as the lofty headlands of a dim and distant coast are seen from the sea; though more clearly stated in the New Testament. But the distant view is not without grandeur and importance. And as the best, and in fact the only way to remove darkness from a room, is to let in light, so it seems to us the best, if not the only way to save the Old Testament from rationalism and a Christless interpretation on the one hand, and the extravagancies of pietism on the other, is to promote its true understanding; and in order to this we must vindicate its authenticity and come to its true interpretation. But this cannot be done by *ignoring* altogether the schools of Neological criticism, nor by allegorizing and finding types of Christ in everything. I am perfectly sure that in regard to modern science, historical discoveries, and antiquarian researches, we may rest securely on the position of our distinguished countryman (Lieut. Maury): "I have always found," says he, "in my scientific studies, that when I could get the Bible to say anything upon the subject, it afforded me a firm foundation to stand upon, and another round in the ladder by which I could safely ascend."

Within the last fifty years, and even within less than half that period, wonderful progress has been made in nearly all the branches of sacred literature. Profound grammatical and lexicographical researches have made us better acquainted with the Hebrew and cognate tongues. The customs and institutions of Oriental nations are now quite familiar to us. Ancient writers and monumental records are interpreted with much more accuracy than in ages past. By being able to read the hieroglyphic records of the private and public life of the ancient Egyptians, we know more of "the court of the Pharaohs than we do of the Plantagenets." And these records afford important, though undesigned, confirmations of the historical verity of the Old Testament, and enable us to understand many hitherto obscure Biblical passages and allusions. So numerous and important are the proofs and illustrations of the authenticity of the historical books of the Bible, gathered from the labours of modern missionaries and travellers in the East, and from the readings of the inscriptions on the monuments of the Nile, Tigris, and Euphrates, that our Bible dictionaries and commentaries will all have to be re-written. Many of them have been superseded already. Important as they have been, I hope it will not be considered ungrateful in me to say, that the chief commentaries in our language of a former age, are destitute of the refreshing breath of science, and without the lights of such patient and thorough research into antiquity as characterizes our day. This was rather their misfortune than their fault. While we shall ever thank God for their able and pious labours, it is but true to say, that they wrote sermons *about* rather than *expositions* of the sacred text.

Most of the old commentators are too much given to *spiritualizing* rather than *expounding* the word of God. We cannot have too much of Christ in our pulpits ; but the spirit of our age calls also for historical and critical studies in order to the successful presentation of "Christ and him crucified." And if, in preaching from the sacred *records*, we dismember them, and in our zeal to find evangelical doctrines, fail to apprehend the mind of the Spirit, then we do great injustice to revelation. We should avoid ex tremes, for doubtless there is a way to avail ourselves of the results of modern criticism, so as to combine the orthodox faith of former ages with the science and ripened fruits of modern times. The wonderful discoveries of our day furnish such a weight of evidence in favour of the historic realities and accuracy of the divine records and of the literal fulfilment of prophecy, that they actually form a new and extensive class of Evidences for Christianity. These discoveries are, however, so recent, and so diversified and scattered, that they can hardly be said yet to be classified or arranged. Nor is this species of evidence by any means complete. But enough is known to convince candid and intelligent readers that the ancient historians and monumental records of the East do furnish us with remarkable illustrations of the sacred writers, and undesigned coincidences so striking, so numerous, and so minute, that it is difficult to escape from the conviction that the Bible books are both genuine and authentic. Let it be kept, however, distinctly in mind, that in the following pages there is no attempt to go over the whole field just referred to. By no means. I have not travelled out of the sacred record concerning Samson. I have only attempted to sum up and arrange together so much of the results of biblical researches as seemed to me to belong to the life of the Israelitish judge. I am aware, moreover, that views and objections bearing upon the "Book of Judges" and the life of Samson have been put forth by Rosenmuller, Eichhorn, Maurer, Paulus, Strauss, and others, adverse to those defended in these pages, which I have not thought of sufficient importance or pertinency to be named at all, lest it should seem to the sturdy, honest Bible readers of our own country that we were fighting men of straw. And besides, if we have succeeded in vindicating and making good our interpretations, theirs must fall to the ground.

I do not suppose it is a valid objection against publishing a book that other volumes on the same subject have preceded it. For every man has his *own* anointing, and no one else can do the work to which providence has called him. Many valuable commentaries and volumes of Bible Illustrations have been published, and those named in the following pages are especially recommended, with the hope that if they are not already in every library and family, they soon will be. It is but justice to say, however, that I am not acquainted with a single work on the plan of this one, or that occupies the place it is designed to fill. In the preparation of these chapters, I have endeavoured, if I may so express myself, to saturate my mind and heart with the spirit of the original text, and with the writings of the most approved critics and interpreters of it, and, as far as I was able, to exhaust them in whatever I deemed available for explaining and presenting in a brief way the true meaning of the narrative. I suppose it to be the duty of every conscientious interpreter of the word of God to study it, as the old divines express it, *painfully*, and to use freely the best helps within reach, for enabling them to show the people the way of salvation. The Hebrew has been carefully studied; but as Hebrew Bibles are now within reach of all who desire to see the original, we have not printed it in our pages. We thought it best to present the edifice with as few signs of the *scaffolding* as were sufficient to give an idea how it was built.

The collection of facts and customs from Bible Lands used as illustrations of the text have in most cases been verified by my own personal researches and observations in the East, and by the latest readings of oriental monuments, so far as they have any bearing on our narrative. I have sought to remove objections, and to bring home the truth. My aim is the conversion of the heart to God by pouring light upon it. And if it shall please God to bless the undertaking, to HIM be all the praise, through Jesus Christ. Amen.

# THE GIANT JUDGE.

## CHAPTER I.

### THE HERO'S STORY TOLD.

"Jewish history is God's illuminated clock set in the dark steeple of time."

"Most wondrous book! bright candle of the Lord!
Star of Eternity! The only star
By which the bark of man could navigate
The sea of life, and gain the coast of bliss
Securely."

JUDGES xiii—xvi.—And the children of Israel did evil again in the sight of the Lord; and the Lord delivered them into the hand of the Philistines forty years.

And there was a certain man of Zorah, of the family of the Danites, whose name was Manoah; and his wife was barren, and bare not. And the angel of the Lord appeared unto the woman, and said unto her, Behold now, thou art barren, and bearest not: but thou shalt conceive, and bear a son. Now therefore beware, I pray thee, and drink not wine nor strong drink, and eat not any unclean thing: for, lo, thou shalt conceive, and bear a son; and no razor shall come on his head: for the child shall be a Nazarite unto God from the womb; and he shall begin to deliver Israel out of the hand of the Philistines. Then the woman came and told her husband, saying, A man of God came unto me, and his countenance was like the countenance of an angel of God, very terrible: but I asked him not whence he was, neither told he me his name: but he said unto me, Behold, thou shalt conceive, and bear a son; and now drink no wine nor strong drink, neither eat any unclean thing: for the child shall be a Nazarite to God from the womb to the day of his death.

Then Manoah entreated the Lord, and said, O my Lord, let the man of God which thou didst send come again unto us, and teach us what we shall do unto the child that shall be born. And God hearkened to the voice of Manoah; and the angel of God came again unto the woman as she sat in the field: but Manoah her husband was not with her. And the woman made haste, and ran, and shewed her husband, and said unto him, Behold, the man hath appeared unto me, that came unto me the other day. And Manoah arose, and went after his wife, and came to the man, and said unto him, Art thou the man that spakest unto the woman? And he said, I am. And Manoah said, Now let thy words come to pass. How shall we order the child, and how shall we do unto him? And the angel of the Lord said unto Manoah, Of all that I said unto the woman let her beware. She may not eat of any thing that cometh of the vine, neither let her drink wine or strong drink, nor eat any unclean thing: all that I commanded her let her observe. And Manoah said unto the angel of the Lord, I pray thee, let us detain thee, until we shall have made ready a kid for thee. And the angel of the Lord said unto Manoah, Though thou detain me, I will not eat of thy bread: and if thou wilt offer a burnt-offering, thou must offer it unto the Lord. For Manoah knew not that he was an angel of the Lord. And Manoah said unto the angel of the Lord, What is thy me, that when thy sayings come to pass we may do thee honour? And the angel of the Lord said unto him, Why askest thou thus after my name, seeing it is secret? So Manoah took a kid with a meat-offering, and offered it upon a rock unto the Lord: and the angel did wondrously; and Manoah and his wife looked on. For it came to pass, when the flame went up toward heaven from off the altar, that the angel of the Lord ascended in the flame of the altar. And Manoah and his wife looked on it, and fell on their faces to the ground. But the angel of the Lord did no more appear to Manoah and to his wife. Then Manoah knew that he was an angel of the Lord. And Manoah said unto his wife, We shall surely die, because we have seen God. But his wife said unto him, If the Lord were pleased to kill us, he would not have received a burnt-offering and a meat-offering at our hands, neither would he have shewed us all these things, nor would as at this time have told us such things as these.

And the woman bare a son, and called his name Samson; and the child grew, and the Lord blessed him. And the Spirit of the Lord began to move him at times in the camp of Dan between Zorah and Eshtaol.

And Samson went down to Timnath, and saw a woman in Timnath of the daughters of the Philistines. And he came up, and told his father and his mother, and said, I have seen a woman in Timnath of the daughters of the Philistines: now therefore get her for me to wife. Then his father and his mother said unto him, Is there never a woman among the daughters of thy brethren, or among all my people, that thou goest to take a wife of the uncircumcised Philistines? And Samson said unto his father, Get her for me; for she pleaseth me well. But his father and his mother knew not that it was of the Lord, that he sought an occasion against the Philistines: for at that time the Philistines had dominion over Israel. Then went Samson down, and his father and his mother to Timnath, and came to the vineyards of Timnath: and, behold, a young lion roared against him. And the Spirit of the Lord came mightily upon him, and he rent him as he would have rent a kid, and he had nothing in his hand: but he told not his father or his mother what he had done. And he went down and talked with the woman; and she pleased Samson well.

And after a time he returned to take her, and he turned aside to see the carcass of the lion: and, behold, there was a swarm of bees and honey in the carcass of the lion. And he took thereof in his hands and went on eating, and came to his father and mother, and he gave them, and they did eat: but he told not them that he had taken the honey out of the carcass of the lion. So his father went down unto the woman: and Samson made there a feast; for so used the young men to do. And it came to pass, when they saw him, that they brought thirty companions to be with him. And Samson said unto them, I will now put forth a riddle unto you: if ye can certainly declare it me within the seven days of the feast, and find it out, then I will give you thirty sheets and thirty change of garments: But if ye cannot declare it me, then shall ye give me thirty sheets and thirty change of garments. And they said unto him, Put forth thy riddle, that we may hear it. And he said unto them, Out of the eater came forth meat, and out of the strong came forth sweetness. And they could not in three days expound the riddle. And it came to pass on the seventh day, that they said unto Samson's wife, Entice thy husband that he may declare unto us the riddle, lest we burn thee and thy father's house with fire: have ye called us to take that we have? is it not so? And Samson's wife wept before him, and said, Thou dost but hate me, and lovest me not; thou hast put forth a riddle unto the children of my people, and hast not told it me. And he said unto her,

Behold, I have not told it my father nor my mother, and shall I tell it thee? And she wept before him the seven days, while their feast lasted: and it came to pass on the seventh day, that he told her, because she lay sore upon him: and she told the riddle to the children of her people. And the men of the city said unto him on the seventh day before the sun went down, What is sweeter than honey? and what is stronger than a lion? And he said unto them, If ye had not plowed with my heifer, ye had not found out my riddle. And the Spirit of the Lord came upon him, and he went down to Ashkelon, and slew thirty men of them and took their spoil, and gave change of garments unto them which expounded the riddle. And his anger was kindled, and he went up to his father's house. But Samson's wife was given to his companion, whom he had used as his friend.

But it came to pass within a while after, in the time of wheat harvest, that Samson visited his wife with a kid; and he said, I will go in to my wife into the chamber. But her father would not suffer him to go in. And her father said, I verily thought that thou hadst utterly hated her; therefore I gave her to thy companion: is not her younger sister fairer than she? take her, I pray thee, instead of her.

And Samson said concerning them, Now shall I be more blameless than the Philistines, though I do them a displeasure. And Samson went and caught three hundred foxes, and took firebrands, and turned tail to tail, and put a firebrand in the midst between two tails. And when he had set the brands on fire, he let them go into the standing corn of the Philistines, and burnt up both the shocks, and also the standing corn, with the vineyards and olives. Then the Philistines said, Who hath done this? And they answered, Samson, the son-in-law of the Timnite, because he had taken his wife, and given her to his companion. And the Philistines came up, and burnt her and her father with fire.

And Samson said unto them, Though ye have done this, yet will I be avenged of you, and after that I will cease. And he smote them hip and thigh with a great slaughter: and he went down and dwelt in the top of the rock Etam.

Then the Philistines went up, and pitched in Judah, and spread themselves in Lehi. And the men of Judah said, Why are ye come up against us? And they answered, To bind Samson are we come up, to do to him as he hath done to us. Then three thousand men of Judah went to the top of the rock Etam, and said to Samson, Knowest thou not that the Philistines are rulers over us? What is this that thou hast done unto us? And he said unto them, As they did unto me, so have I done unto them. And they said unto him, We are come down to bind thee, that we may deliver thee into the hand of the Philistines. And Samson said unto them, Swear unto me, that ye will not fall upon me yourselves. And they spake unto him, saying, No; but we will bind thee fast, and deliver thee into their hand: but surely we will not kill thee. And they bound him with two new cords, and brought him up from the rock.

And when he came unto Lehi, the Philistines shouted against him: and the Spirit of the Lord came mightily upon him, and the cords that were upon his arms became as flax that was burnt with fire, and his bands loosed from off his hands. And he found a new jawbone of an ass, and put forth his hand and took it, and slew a thousand men therewith. And Samson said, With the jawbone of an ass, heaps upon heaps, with the jaw of an ass have I slain a thousand men. And it came to pass, when he had made an end of speaking, that he cast away the jawbone out of his hand, and called that place Ramath-lehi.

And he was sore athirst, and called on the Lord and

said, Thou hast given this great deliverance into the hand of thy servant: and now shall I die for thirst, and fall into the hand of the uncircumcised? But God clave an hollow place that was in the jaw, and there came water thereout; and when he had drunk, his spirit came again, and he revived: wherefore he called the name thereof En-hak-kore, which is in Lehi unto this day. And he judged Israel in the days of the Philistines twenty years.

Then went Samson to Gaza, and saw there an harlot, and went in unto her. And it was told the Gazites, saying, Samson is come hither. And they compassed him in, and laid wait for him all night in the gate of the city, and were quiet all the night, saying, In the morning, when it is day, we shall kill him. And Samson lay till midnight, and arose at midnight, and took the doors of the gate of the city, and the two posts, and went away with them, bar and all, and put them upon his shoulders, and carried them up to the top of an hill that is before Hebron.

And it came to pass afterwards, that he loved a woman in the valley of Sorek, whose name was Delilah. And the lords of the Philistines came up unto her, and said unto her, Entice him, and see wherein his great strength lieth, and by what means we may prevail against him, that we may bind him to afflict him: and we will give thee every one of us eleven hundred pieces of silver. And Delilah said to Samson, Tell me, I pray thee, wherein thy great strength lieth, and wherewith thou mightest be bound to afflict thee. And Samson said unto her, If they bind me with seven green withs that were never dried, then shall I be weak, and be as another man. Then the lords of the Philistines brought up to her seven green withs which had not been dried, and she bound him with them. Now there were men lying in wait, abiding with her in the chamber. And she said unto him, The Philistines be upon thee, Samson. And he brake the withs, as a thread of tow is broken when it toucheth the fire. So his strength was not known. And Delilah said unto Samson, Behold, thou hast mocked me, and told me lies: now tell me, I pray thee, wherewith thou mightest be bound. And he said unto her, If they bind me fast with new ropes that never were occupied, then shall I be weak, and be as another man. Delilah therefore took new ropes, and bound him therewith, and said unto him, The Philistines be upon thee, Samson. And there were liers in wait abiding in the chamber. And he brake them from off his arms like a thread. And Delilah said unto Samson, Hitherto thou hast mocked me, and told me lies: tell me wherewith thou mightest be bound. And he said unto her, If thou weavest the seven locks of my head with the web. And she fastened it with the pin, and said unto him, The Philistines be upon thee, Samson. And he awaked out of his sleep, and went away with the pin of the beam, and with the web. And she said unto him, How canst thou say, I love thee, when thine heart is not with me? Thou hast mocked me these three times, and hast not told me wherein thy great strength lieth. And it came to pass, when she pressed him daily with her words, and urged him, so that his soul was vexed unto death, that he told her all his heart, and said unto her, There hath not come a razor upon mine head; for I have been a Nazarite unto God from my mother's womb: if I be shaven, then my strength will go from me, and I shall become weak, and be like any other man. And when Delilah saw that he had told her all his heart, she sent and called for the lords of the Philistines, saying, Come up this once, for he hath shewed me all his heart. Then the lords of the Philistines came up unto her, and brought money in their hand. And she made him sleep upon her knees; and she called for a man, and she caused him to shave off the seven locks of his head; and she began to afflict him, and his strength went from him. And she said, The Philistines be upon thee, Samson. And he awoke out of his sleep, and said, I will go out as at other times before, and shake myself. And he wist not that the Lord was departed from him. But the Philistines took him and put out his eyes, and brought him down to Gaza, and bound him with fetters of brass; and he did grind in the prison-house.

Howbeit the hair of his head began to grow again after he was shaven. Then the lords of the Philistines gathered them together for to offer a great sacrifice unto Dagon their god, and to rejoice; for they said, Our god hath delivered Samson our enemy into our hand. And when the people saw him, they praised their god: for they said, Our god hath delivered into our hands our enemy, and the destroyer of our country, which slew many of us. And it came to pass, when their hearts were merry, that they said, Call for Samson, that he may make us sport. And they called for Samson out of the prison-house; and he made them sport: and they set him between the pillars. And Samson said unto the lad that held him by the hand, Suffer me that I may feel the pillars whereupon the house standeth, that I may lean upon them. Now the house was full of men and women; and all the lords of the Philistines were there; and there were upon the roof about three thousand men and women, that beheld while Samson made sport. And Samson called unto the Lord, and said, O Lord God, remember me, I pray thee, and strengthen me, I pray thee, only this once, O God, that I may be at once avenged of the Philistines for my two eyes. And Samson took hold of the two middle pillars upon which the house stood, and on which it was borne up, of the one with his right hand, and of the other with his left. And Samson said, Let me die with the Philistines. And he bowed himself with all his might;

and the house fell upon the lords, and upon all the people that were therein. So the dead which he slew at his death were more than they which he slew in his life. Then his brethren and all the house of his father came down, and took him and brought him up, and buried him between Zorah and Eshtaol in the burying-place of Manoah his father. And he judged Israel twenty years.

# CHAPTER II.

## THE HEROIC JUDGES AND THEIR TIMES.

"Know ye the land where the cypress and myrtle,
Are emblems of deeds that were done in their clime,
Where the rage of the vulture, the love of the turtle,
Now melt into sorrow, now madden to crime?"

*Bride of Abydos.*

And what shall I more say? for the time would fail me to tell of Gideon, and of Barak, and of Samson, and of Jephthah; of David also, and Samuel, and of the prophets: who through faith subdued kingdoms, wrought righteousness. * * * * And these all, having obtained a good report through faith, received not the promise: God having provided some better thing for us, that they without us should not be made perfect.—Heb. xi. 32-40.

As the life and exploits of Israel's GIANT JUDGE are described in "the Book of Judges," and as he was himself one of the most remarkable of this extraordinary class of men, it may be well to say something of these heroic Judges and of their times. Their history is an important link in Israel's ancient story. For though some of the facts here recorded seem not to have a direct religious interest, still as fragments of family and national history, they are exceedingly valuable. It was important, at least until the Messiah should come, to preserve the distinctive tribal lines and history of the Hebrews. And even in our times, apparently unimportant facts recorded in the earlier books of the Bible have been of great value in ethnology and philology, and for the general history of mankind.

In the history of the Judges, we have a striking picture of the disorder and dangers of a country without a well established government. In those days when the people had no "vision," that is, when they were without prophets to instruct them; and when there was no government, but "every one did that which was right in his own eyes:"—then, "the highways were unoccupied, and the travellers walked through by-ways." There is no liberty, where there is no law. There is no protection for property "throughout the purple land, where law secures not life."

The Hebrew word *Shophetim*, Judges, is from the verb *to judge, discern, command, rule, execute punishment.* In the East, judging and ruling were generally connected. And sitting in judgment is still one of the principal duties of an oriental sovereign. The term Judges, when used in the Bible in reference to those heroes that God raised up between the days of Joshua and David to be the saviours of their country, is equivalent to Rulers. And this is the common use of the term Judges, in the days of Samson, and up to the gift of a King. It appears from the life of Samuel, however, and also from Judges iv. 5, that these Judges did sometimes act as judges merely, and not as judges and executioners of their own sentences. The main idea then of these Judges is not the literal one of a judge seated on a judicial bench, and pronouncing the sentence of the law in criminal cases. They were chief magistrates. The Judge for the time being was the head of the nation. Jehovah was the King; the government was a Theocracy, and the Judges were his Lieutenant Generals, or his Deputies.

The Judges of Israel were, however, neither hereditary, nor chosen by the people. They were in every case raised up on some extraordinary occasion to execute some divine judgment upon Israel's wicked oppressors, or to fulfil some specific mission. They kept no court, had no standing army, and received no pay. They had neither the pomp, nor the ceremony usually attached to the head of a State. Nor had they the power to make any new laws, nor to change the old ones. Their mission was altogether a peculiar, a distinctive one. In the history of civil rulers they stand out in solitary prominence as Melchisedec does in the history of the priesthood. Their only authority was to execute the laws, and effect such deliverance of the chosen people from their heathen oppressors as God himself should direct. Officially, they were without father or mother and without offspring. They had no predecessors, and they left no successors.

The government of the Judges continued about four hundred and fifty years. And if Samuel be considered as a prophet as well as a judge, and Eli a priest as well as a judge, we may consider Samson as the last of that peculiar order of governors. Samuel, it is true, judged Israel, but he did not begin to act as a judge till forty years of age, and during the greater part of that time, Saul was king. It is, therefore, with much propriety, that the "first book of Samuel is otherwise called the first book of Kings." The history of Samson occupies four out of the twenty chapters of the book of Judges, and is more fully written out than that of any of the others. His history is surprising even in an extraordinary age. In several particulars he was the most distinguished of the Hebrew Judges. And though never at the head of an army, nor on a throne, nor prime minister to any earthly potentate, it were difficult, perhaps impossible, to name another Hebrew that loved his country with more fervid devotion, or served it with a more hearty good will, or who was a greater terror to its enemies. I know not that there is any biography so completely characteristic, or more tragical than his. It is full of stirring incidents and most marvellous achievements. His whole life consists of a good beginning pre-announced, and a relapse from early piety into a long, dark, and terrible conflict, in which we find a mother's piety and a father's faith in battle array with constitutional and besetting sins; but at last they prevail, and the sun that shone on him in his youth shines on him in his old age and gilds his dying exploits with terrible glory. He seems to us like a volcano, continually struggling for an eruption. In him we have all the elements of an epic; love, adventure, heroism, tragedy. Nor am I aware that any Bible character has lent to modern literature a greater amount of metaphor and comparison than the story of Samson. The "Samson Agonistes" of Milton has been pronounced by the highest authority to be "one of the noblest dramas in the English language." It reminds us of the mystic touches and shadowy grandeur of Rembrandt, while Rembrandt himself and Rubens, Guido, David, and Martin are indebted to this heroic Judge for several of their immortal pieces.

I am aware that some look upon Samson merely as a strong man, just as they do upon Solomon as a wise man; but find nothing supernatural in either. They forget that it was the special inspiration of the Almighty that taught Solomon wisdom above all other men. They do not consider that the moving of the Spirit of Jehovah gave extraordinary strength to Samson for special purposes. It does not appear that his stature or limbs were of gigantic proportions. His strength, on the contrary, was "hung in his hair," the weakest part of his physical frame, to show that it was the special gift of God. It is, therefore, wholly in regard to his strength, I have called him the "Giant Judge of Israel." His peculiarities are not remarkable, because of any thing that we perceive foreign to fallen humanity in the kind or composition of his passions and besetting sins, but in the fierceness and greatness of their strength. Saul, the son of Kish, was of the people and among them—he was of their flesh and bones;—but he was a head and shoulders above them. It is just so with Samson. Ordinary men now have the same besetting sins—passions of the same character, but they are diminutive in comparison with him, and are without his supernatural strength.

It must be confessed in the outset, that Samson's spiritual history is very skeleton-like. We have only a few time-worn fragments out of which to construct his inner man. Now and then, and sometimes after long and dreary intervals, and from out of heavy clouds and thick darkness, we catch a few rays of hope, and rejoice in some signs of a reviving conscience and of the presence of God's Spirit. Possibly no part of the Bible has given occasion for more raillery than the book of Judges. And perhaps no name in that book has given point to more infidel jests than that of Samson. "His character is indeed dark and almost inexplicable. By none of the Judges of Israel did God work so many miracles, and yet by none were so many faults committed." As no Bible hero is so remarkable for strength, so none are so remarkable for weakness, as Samson. His faults and passions were like himself. The Apostle, however, in Hebrews xi, settles the question as to his personal piety and salvation at last, by enrolling him in the list of heroes distinguished for faith and glorious deeds. But as an old writer has said, he must be looked upon as "rather a rough believer." A recent Scotch author (Rev. Dr. Bruce in his biography of Samson) divides his life into three periods. The *first*, his youth, when all was prosperous and he was truly pious. This period extends to his marriage, when his *second* period begins, which is marked by his fall, and is very dark. In which period, like David, he made sad shipwreck of the faith—"and strangely enough from the very same blinding, and beguiling, and peculiarly brutalizing lust; and yet like David also, and some others, he escaped at the last as by a hair's breadth—the Lord forgiveth his iniquity, whilst yet he took vengeance on his inventions." The *third* period he denominates the period of his penitence, recovery, and triumphant death. This period, the revival of his graces and gifts as a child of God, begins with the growing of his hair in the prison. This author dwells chiefly upon Samson's history as an illustration of christian experience. He endeavours to illustrate the continual struggle between good and evil in the human soul, sometimes the one predominating, and then again the other, the evil drawing down its own punishment, and the good at last prevailing. He makes Samson a striking instance of "the delivery of the body to Satan for the destruction of the flesh, that the spirit may be saved in the day of the Lord Jesus." Now it is undoubtedly true, that the strugglings of "this mighty and marvellous Israelite," with his wild passions and his better resolutions—his conflicts with most hurtful lusts and convictions of duty, do well illustrate the Apostle's warfare between the flesh and the spirit; but it may be fairly questioned whether this is the main design of his history, as it is given to us. According to Dr. Bruce, Samson was not so much a type of Christ, as of the conscience of a believer quickened by his Spirit, and contending for the mastery over those carnal passions which are well represented by the tyrant and treacherous Philistines. I like not to dwell on Samson as a type of Christ. We must at least guard against removing him so far from us by reason of his uniqueness of character, as to forget that he was a man of like passions with ourselves. We must carefully discriminate in his life between what God moved him to do, and what his sinful passions moved him to. I fear a disposition to neglect the Old Testament characterizes our times. True indeed, most people in christendom suppose themselves well acquainted with the character of Samson. They at least know he is called the strongest man, and that he killed a lion, slept in Delilah's lap, and killed a great many Philistines at his death. This they may know, and yet not be able to form a true estimate of his character, or draw from his history those important lessons, which it teaches. Doubtless many have read Samson's history just as they do that of "the Scottish Chiefs," or of King Philip. They have found in Samson the wonderful deeds of an Ishmaelite, ever ready for a border fray, fiery and fierce, and of extraordinary strength, and nothing more. This were to lose very much of what the Holy Spirit certainly designed us to learn from this memoir. The Lord raised up this heroic Israelite for us. He threw into him a miraculous composition of strength and energy of passion, and called them forth in such a way as to make him our teacher. And besides being a hero, he was a believer, a child of God, a member of the body of Christ, his church, which is his kingdom. God raised him up for our learning, and made him, as it were, "a mirror or molten looking-glass," in which we may see some of our own leading features truthfully portrayed, only on an enlarged scale. And if we differ from him, or from other great sinners, who but God hath made us to differ? If in any thing we are not so bad as others, it is not owing to ourselves, but to the sovereign grace of God.

Let it be remembered, in studying such a biography as this of the Giant Judge of Israel, that we should not expect, and could not indeed have, any other than one that records infirmities and short comings, as well as virtues and heroic deeds. Samson was a man—a sinful man. His life and exploits are recorded in an honest, truth-telling memoir. This point comes up again in the next chapter in considering the design and method upon which the earlier biblical memoirs were written.

It is not to be inferred then by any means, that in making

mention of Samson, the Apostle approved of all that he did. Nor indeed of any of the other champions of faith whom he names. All that he commends is his faith. All that he here speaks of is the faith of the ancients. It was not his purpose to give a full account of these worthies. He was not writing their history. He was not called upon in this connection to speak of their imperfections; but to show that however great their faults may have been, they were remarkable for their confidence in God. By reciting this muster roll of the old champions of faith, the Apostle sought to awaken the courage of the Hebrew believers of his day, by bidding them remember what faith had achieved for men and women like them in ages past.

"All these," the apostle says, "obtained a good report through faith." That is, on account of their confidence in God. They were accepted of him, and are commended by all the pious. The procuring cause of pardon and acceptance from the beginning, was the blood of the Lamb, slain from the foundation of the world. This they received by faith—not the reality, but the promise. They believed the promise as if it were fulfilled. They did not actually see its fulfilment, but they did look forward in perfect confidence to its fulfilment, and consequently received the blessings promised as if the great promise had actually been fulfilled.

Lives of great men all remind us
  We can make our lives sublime,
And departing, leave behind us
  Footprints on the sand of time.
Footprints that perhaps another,
  Sailing o'er life's solemn main,
A forlorn and shipwrecked brother,
  Seeing, shall take heart again.
Let us, then, be up and doing,
  With a heart for any fate;
Still achieving, still pursuing,
  Learn to labour and to wait.

*Longfellow's Psalm of Life.*

# CHAPTER III.

## THE STORY A REVELATION INSPIRED.

"This book,—this glorious book, on every line
Marked with the seal of high Divinity;
On every leaf bedewed with drops of love
Divine."———

Holy men of God spake as they were moved by the Holy Ghost.—
2 Pet. i. 21.

All scripture is given by inspiration of God, and is profitable for doctrine, for reproof, for correction, for instruction in righteousness; that the man of God [a christian man] may be perfect, thoroughly furnished unto all good works.—2 Tim. iii. 16, 17.

It is not the purpose of this chapter to consider the evidences of christianity in general, nor to offer proofs of the inspiration of God in the Bible. Our undertaking is a more limited one. In the previous chapters, we have a wonderful story of heroic times. And though it is remarkable even in a collection of marvellous records, still it belongs to a series of biographies that we are accustomed to look upon with great reverence. In so far then as we may be able to explain in what sense the recorded story of the life and exploits of Israel's Giant Judge is a revelation from God, made in a supernatural way, and transferred to human language by an extraordinary or miraculous degree of inspiration, we shall not only justify the reverence with which we are wont to treat this sacred story, but establish the claims of all the Bible biographies to a like respect. The story then, in hand, of the heroic Hebrew Judge—is it an inspired record, and on what plan, and for what purpose were such biblical memoirs written? It is proper to consider these questions, since there are those who still assert that the Old Testament is either totally unconnected with the New, except by a mere chance, or that it has ceased to be of any importance. This assertion argues either ignorance, or a false conception of spiritual christianity, or an inordinate zeal to support certain dogmatic views of religion. Still it is thrust upon us so often and with so much urgency, that it is well for us to consider the place of Bible biographies, especially of the earlier times, in the history of mankind.

Why should we then as christians study the Old Testament?

I. In answering this question, it were perhaps enough to say, that the doctrines and precepts, principles and duties which are taught in and illustrated by the lives of Bible characters, are found to be the best manual in existence for developing and strengthening, refining, elevating, and giving expansion to our mental faculties. There is nothing equal to the theology of the Bible to strengthen and purify the human mind. The divinity of the Scottish Knox has given breadth and power to the Scottish mind. He gave Scotland her schools and an open Bible, and Scotland has well improved his gifts. It is "from scenes like these," so touchingly described in the Cotter's Saturday Night,—"Old Scotia's grandeur springs, that makes her loved at home, revered abroad." And the Cotter's Saturday Night reminds us that the late Mr. Hugh Miller, in one of his essays, which are his ablest productions, quotes with approbation, the remark of Gilbert Burns, brother of the poet, that "it was not from the parish school that the people of Scotland derived their higher education, but from the parish pulpits. It was to their ministers, not to their schoolmasters, that the Scotch owed both their sober and their severe thinking." "Never," continues Mr. Miller, "was the strong common sense of Gilbert Burns, which was as much a gift of nature as the genius of his brother, more unequivocally manifested than in his remark on the real source, whence the Scotch people had derived of old the tone of high moral sentiment by which they were characterized, and their severe semi-metaphysical cast of thinking. An earnest Calvinistic ministry had been their real teachers. We well remember a class of intelligent and thoughtful men, now nearly all passed away, who had received their only teaching from the church and from the Bible; nor can we avoid regretting, when we think how much they formed the salt of the Scottish people, that the class should be so well nigh an extinct one. The pabulum on which they fed and grew strong still survives, however; and when we hear from the pulpit, powerful and original thinking that awakens thought in others, while at the same time it ensures the diffusion of an element of earnestness, we recognize in it the old teaching, which made the people of Scotland what they were when at their best." Yes, the pabulum still survives and if we mistake not, the class so much admired by the geologist is by no means "an extinct one." There are those, and not a few, in his country and in our own, who still adhere to "the old way of teaching"—who read and expound the word of God, and cause the people to understand its meaning.

It is no doubt true that the influence the pulpit once had almost entirely to itself, is now shared with the Sabbath-school, the colporteur, and the printing press; still the "power of the pulpit" in preventing crime, and in promoting virtue and religion, is very great. Like the life-giving principle of the air, it is everywhere, and yet scarcely recognized. Doubtless there is much inefficiency in the pulpit, but is there none in the pews? But few ministers of the gospel are as able and successful as they should be, but are the hearers of the word efficient doers? The main business of the pulpit is to bring the Divine word *home* to the conscience—into living contact with the mind and heart of the hearers. And if we are not greatly mistaken, the best way to do this, is "the old way of teaching," that is, of teaching the people as the prophets and apostles and our blessed Lord himself taught them. Doctrines, precepts, promises, threatenings, commands, and duties are taught in the scriptures by biographies, or memoirs and parables. The chequered life of man is made to teach and illustrate what we are to believe and what we are to do, that we may inherit eternal life. The biographies of the Bible are living lessons. They are not perfect as pictures, but true to the life, giving the blemishes as well as the beauties. The Judges of Israel, and all the heroes that lived before and since Agamemnon are nothing to us, unless we recognize them to be "men of like passions with ourselves"—"our loftier brothers, but one in blood." To read or preach of the thousands who have lived before us, "in the gray dawn of time," as if we were reciting some unmeaning hearsay story, is to fail altogether of a proper appreciation of the mind of the Spirit in causing the biographies of the Bible to be written. The Hebrew historians, by one single touch, one little incident, chronicle the state of a man's mind or a period of his life, and expose at one view the naked anatomy of the human heart. There are no such biographical memoirs anywhere else as we have in the Bible. As studies of the natural history of man's inner life, they challenge our highest attention. It is for us to draw warning and encouragement from the lives of holy men of old, who did battle for the right, both against themselves and the world, and who sometimes fell, and then, after many a struggle, rose again to the conflict, and after a life-long quarrel with sin and the enemies of God, gloriously triumphed. If we read their lives aright, as we work at the "flaming forge of life," we shall

> "Know how sublime a thing it is
> To suffer and be strong."

A studied depreciation of the scriptures of the Old Testament has ever marked the course of rationalism in the old world, and is one of the most unfavourable symptoms of the theological movements of our own country, especially of New England, under the lead of such men as Parker and Emerson. It is not enough to take out of them all true evangelism. The inspiration of the prophets is made nothing more than the inspiration of genius, such as is common to an artist, a poet, or an orator. On the contrary we hold that the scriptures are of God in the highest sense of inspiration, and that they testify of Christ and of eternal life through him. Some heretics in ancient times held that the Old Testament was the work of a secondary evil principle or deity, that was in perpetual warfare with the eternal fountain of good.*

---

* Marcion and his followers rejected the Old Testament altogether. Schleiermacher and his school deny its inspiration. Some of them even go so far as to say that "an owl is as much inspired as Isaiah was." They all contend that there is no higher inspiration than "christian consciousness." It is obvious whither all this tends. The result is the same, whether we rely on man's "inner light," "religious sentiment," "religious intentions," "spiritual insight," or "christian consciousness." If these or any of them be supreme, then the writings of the prophets and apostles are no more inspired than are the recorded views and feelings of Bunyan and Payson, or of christians generally. And if so, we are without any infallible rule of faith and manners. What we have regarded as a revelation supernaturally made is nothing better than the light of nature. Indeed, *natural* and *revealed* religion become to us one and the same. The English and the French deists of the last century were but little, if at all, further from the truth, than Newman and Parker, and the Neologists of Germany in general.

According to this view the Jewish system was to be regarded as essentially defective and positively evil—carnal and debasing. Consequently Christ came not to fulfil, but to destroy—and in fact, the New Testament is something wholly new, different from, and in contradiction to, the Old Testament. On the other hand, some of the first converts from Judaism to christianity, insisted on the continued obligations of the law of Moses, not only on converted Jews, but also on converted Gentiles. They insisted on circumcision as well as baptism—on obedience to Moses as well as to Christ in order to salvation. This error the great apostle, who wrote the epistle to the Hebrews, has most happily corrected, and so corrected as to show us the use of, and the difference between, the two dispensations.

SPENCER* and his followers rob the Old Testament of its christianity, and not a few evangelical authors on the other side have betrayed an inclination to over-estimate the perfection of the Mosaic dispensation. Some have found no types of Christ, no resurrection, no immortality in the Old Testament; others spiritualize almost everything in it.

Both extremes are to be avoided. Ever since the days of ORIGEN, the cause of truth has been more or less embarrassed by allegorical interpretations of scripture. The fault, in our judgment, of many evangelical writers is that they find types, where, oftentimes, we should be taught only by suggestion, or by way of accommodation. A too liberal or a too literal rule of interpretation may be alike erroneous. If the Protestant enhances the distinction between the law and the gospel, the Romanist underrates it. And both have

* See Spencer's work De Legibus Hebrœorum. In answer to him see Witsius on the Covenants, lib. iv. c. 11, 12. Also Calvin's Institutes, lib. ii. c. 10. While it is certainly a great error to rob the Old Testament of its christianity, it is an error of not less magnitude to despoil the distinctive doctrines of the New Testament, by unduly pressing analogies and types out of the Old upon the New.

a theory to support, or dogmatical prepossessions to defend. The true view is, that the law is a schoolmaster to bring us to Christ, who fulfilled the law and the prophets, and by one offering of himself hath perfected for ever them that are sanctified. See Heb. x. 12—14.

There are types as well as prophecies, in the Old Testament. But every incident or word of it is not so to be interpreted. The Mosaic economy was typical and preparatory to the gospel. But the minutiæ of the temple, the nails and badgers' skins of the tabernacle, and many such things, were not types. A brave man is compared to a lion; but it were ridiculous to press the analogy, and figure out his resemblance to a lion, and find the counterpart of the lion's mane and claws. An indifference to revealed truth, if not to spiritual religion, lies at the bottom of this depreciation of the Old Testament. For no book of the Bible is a mere dry statement of the past. They are all instinct with life. Even the list of hard names is of importance. Genealogical tables are of use in tracing out the promises and verifying their fulfilment. Our only sure guide is the written word of God. We are to listen to what God has said—what doctrines and duties he has taught in the lives of holy men and women in olden times, not as recorded by fabulists, but as recorded by men moved to write by the Holy Spirit. The voice of all antiquity is not the voice of God. The voice of God comes to us with authority only as revealed by his holy prophets and by his own Son, Jesus Christ, and his apostles. He is then but poorly qualified to appreciate the gospel, or to teach it to others as a minister, or Sabbath-school teacher, who is a stranger to the treasury of truth contained in the Old Testament. Nor are the narratives of the Old Testament fit only to instruct adults. They supply the best material for impressing on the mind of childhood the lessons of our holy religion.

We have the authority of an apostle, that whatsoever things were written aforetime by Moses and the prophets were written for our learning. There is no fact recorded in Bible history that has not its echo still. The living world is but the recurring cycles of the past. Many of the actors on the stage of past history, are at this moment exercising a great influence on the world. Hearts long since cold under the green sod have sent out pulsations that are now beating, and will not cease till the sound of the trumpet of the last day. They being dead yet speak—still live by their influence on the acting generation, who will transmit their influence to the generations yet to come. The great and good of all past ages lived for us. Abel suffered for us. Abraham was tried for us. The patriarchs, prophets, lawgivers, and wise men of old, "the noble army of martyrs"—all lived and died for us. Every mother's babe in christendom is at this moment under the influence of the histories of the Bible. Whatsoever was done and said from the beginning, is impressing its influence upon our hearts and actions at this very moment. If this be true in general, as it certainly is, then the biographies of the earlier periods of the Bible are worthy of our serious attention. They reveal the existence and attributes of the Creator, and teach us how men and women like ourselves feared and served God.

II. It is desirable, therefore, in the next place, that we understand on what plan or method, and with what design, these earlier biographies of the Bible were written. We believe there is a God, a personal, a living God, who is a Spirit, infinite and eternal, in contradistinction to "the dead god of deism" and pantheism. We have a God to glorify and enjoy, as well as a soul to save. And to enable us to do this, God has spoken to us. He has come down to us, that we may go up to him. Our Creator has come down to us in various ways and by manifold representations—by appearing to the patriarchs and speaking to them and the prophets in several ways, and last of all, by his Son Jesus Christ. Next to the existence of God in importance to us, is the question of a revelation from him to us as his creatures. If we have no access to him—if there is no communication between us and our Creator, we are of all creatures the most miserable; our higher nature and nobler aspirations are then only to make us susceptible of miseries the brute can never know. But "God, who, at sundry times and in divers manners, spake in times past unto the fathers by the prophets, hath in these last days spoken unto us by his Son, whom he hath appointed heir of all things, by whom also he made the worlds; who is the brightness of his glory, and the express image of his person." In this God-man, the infinite and the finite meet in perfect harmony.

In the Old Testament as well as the New, we have both a revelation from God, and a record in which that revelation is enveloped. God has spoken to us and we have a reliable record of what he has said. Hume and Gibbon, Voltaire, D'Alembert, Diderot, and their associates and followers directed their attacks against christianity itself, but for the last fifty years, the enemies of the Gospel have chiefly aimed to destroy the authority of its written records. They have not busied themselves so much in denying the existence or necessity of revealed religion, as in seeking to destroy all dependence upon its records, or the interpretation of it. They tell us quite patronizingly, revealed religion is desirable. It is a good thing, if we could only know what it is. Now we maintain that we have not merely the idea of christianity in the Bible, but we have christianity itself, and we have a suitable, intelligible record of it, and of what it is. We may not only know that revealed truth is, but we may know what it is.

4

Beyond all controversy, the great question of our day turns upon the interpretation of the Divine word. It is important then for us to be acquainted with the history and proofs of Divine revelation, and to know that the Bible contains that revelation. The unerring message is invested in an infallible record. The Divine Messenger became incarnate in a perfect human organism. The revelation is heavenly, while the record, or history, of it is earthly; but this record was made by Divine direction. And if the Creator has really made a communication to our race, we should have a right to expect that he would take care that it be made in such a way as to embody and bring down to human apprehension just what he had to say to us, and that he would cause such a record of his revelation to be made and preserved, as would make known to the different generations of mankind his will for their salvation. Has God spoken to us? Can we find out exactly what he has said? According to our view, these questions are not to be separated. For it is an impeachment of the Divine wisdom and benevolence to suppose the former without the latter, and the latter of course implies the former. At the risk of repeating, we shall dwell somewhat on these questions. The authority of councils, the orthodoxy of creeds, and the infallibility of popes, are of no consequence in comparison with the subject of inspiration, nor have we any rule by which to settle such questions, until we have found infallibility in the Divine word. If our Creator has not revealed himself to us, we have no religion at all. And if he has revealed himself, but allowed the record of his own revelation to be so made that we cannot know what it is he has revealed, then we are made conscious that there is such a thing as a true religion, and painfully conscious too of our need of it, but left totally unable to find it, or to know certainly what it is. But to make our answer as broad and as direct as our questionings, we say God has spoken from heaven to us, and we may know with as much absolute certainty as we can know anything, both that God has spoken to us and what it is he has said to us. Our Creator has revealed his will to us for our salvation, and we may know what it is, and what that salvation is. In the Bible we have an external revelation, and a real inspiration, and in the teachings of the same Spirit of God by whom this revelation and inspiration have been made, we have also an inward and subjective illumination. The concurrence of faith in the former, with personal experience of the latter, constitutes us true christians.

Revelation and inspiration are distinct; but as we receive these terms, the one implies the other. By a revelation we mean a communication of truth from God to man. By inspiration we mean that the Spirit of God moved the prophets and apostles who received communications from God to write them out, transferring God's thoughts that were put into their minds by his Spirit into human language, and so transferring them as not to mix any error with them, or make any mistake in the use of language. We believe, then, that the Bible is God's own inspired word, and that it is an all-sufficient rule of faith and conduct. It does not follow, however, that all the revelations that God has been pleased to make have been accompanied with the gift of inspiration to make a record of them. If we mistake not, some have had revelations in the highest sense, who did not write them out. And some have been inspired to write, who were endowed with power to work miracles, and yet probably received no revelations themselves. But all the revealed truths of holy scripture have been transferred to human language by the inspiration of God. It seems to us that one of the prolific causes of the confusion that is found in many writers on this subject is the want of distinct and clear statements as to what they mean by revelation and inspiration. Another cause doubtless is that many authors undertake to explain too much, especially as to the *modus* of God's making known his will to us. If we are sure of the fact, may we not rest content in the assurance that Infinite Wisdom employed the right "divers manners," to make communications to our race? We hold therefore that the sacred writers received the truths which they have recorded from God in a supernatural way, and that they were commanded by God himself to make the transcript of these truths for us, and were so directed and assisted in making this transcript by the Holy Spirit, that we have in this transcript not only a true and reliable record of God's thoughts concerning us, but the very thoughts themselves.

The great question then, is not to distinguish between the revelation and the record and history of that revelation, but to get at what the revelation is—what does it reveal? It is of no use to believe that the revelation is itself divine, if its enveloping record is erroneous, for in that case, we can never be sure that we have a revelation of God's will at all. It is to be regretted that so able a writer as Soame Jenyns in exalting the importance of the "Internal Evidences of the Christian Religion," should have thought it necessary to make so marked a distinction between the revelation that God has made to us, and the history we have of that revelation. He contends that we have a heavenly message, but "it is enclosed in a fallible earthly case, by which it is indeed polluted." And yet, he says the human errors and imperfections of the history of this revelation do not affect its divine origin. "A diamond, though found in a bed of mud, is still a diamond, nor can the dirt which surrounds it, depreciate its value or destroy its lustre." In the translation, versions and transcriptions of the ancient writings of the prophets and apostles, and in the different editions of our holy Scriptures, there are verbal inaccuracies. If there were not, they have been prevented by a continued miracle. And it is doubtless true, that the sacred writers have recorded some things that they did not need supernatural influence to be taught them. If Luke has copied his genealogy of the mother of our Lord from the Hebrew tables in common use at Jerusalem or Nazareth, he did not require any other special divine assistance to do it, than to originate the conception of so doing. And Paul could tell his name, and how he had left his cloak and parchments at Troas, without the miraculous guidance of the Holy Ghost. But even in recording such natural events, or circumstances of common life, as they could have recorded if they had not been prophets and apostles, they were so guided and overruled, as to record nothing but what the Holy Spirit saw it best to have recorded for the end in view. We have therefore a revelation from God, and such a record and history of that revelation as God himself caused to be written by his Holy Spirit. The Bible is the word of the one, only, living and true God. We cannot believe that it is "a heap of mummery and priestcraft," nor that the Creator should make a revelation of himself to man, and yet not provide suitably for the communication of that revelation. It is to call in question his sincerity and wisdom, to say that he has revealed certain doctrines for the salvation of mankind, and yet made no provision for an infallibly valid vehicle of that revelation. In the Scriptures, then, of the Old and New Testaments we have the revelation of God, and the record of it, and it is comparatively easy to distinguish and separate the perfect from the imperfect of that record. It surely is no argument against the inspiration of Isaiah, that some words in our translation should be spelled differently in different editions; or that there should be a difference in punctuation and such other minutiæ. The essential integrity of the sacred text has been preserved. The message and the vehicle of the message are from God. What God has revealed has been written for us by his direction. The sacred writers were moved by the Holy Ghost to write as they did. What then have they written, and for what purpose did the Holy Ghost move them to write? The Bible is no more without a design, a plan, and a unity than is the universe. Though composed of two great departments, and of many different books written by different authors, stretching over about two thousand years, and living and writing at different periods and different places, still the Bible is not a series of detached and independent documents, mechanically strung together by the hand of a compiler, nor is it a farrago of heterogeneous fragments accidentally combined. On the contrary, it is a *bona fide* history. It is pervaded from beginning to end by one dominant idea. One great specific purpose is in view from the first word of Genesis to the end of the Revelation of John. On what plan then was the Bible written and for what purpose?

Some tell us that the Old Testament in particular is a collection of romances—that the patriarchs and judges of Israel were mere Bedouin or nomadic chiefs, like the Sheikhs of the modern Arabs, and that the germ of truth was furnished by their lives, which the writer has taken, and worked up after the most approved manner of fiction. The Old Testament, according to this view, is nothing but a biography of some wandering chieftains, written in the style of oriental exaggeration. Some who are ashamed of such a theory as this, modify it, by telling us, the lives of the patriarchs and judges were never meant to be received as true histories at all, but as mere poetical descriptions of life and manners of early times, somewhat after the manner of the Eclogues and Bucolics. What then becomes of the historic memoirs, national festivals commemorative of actual events, and of contemporary and subsequent allusions in the history of other nations, and of the superiority of their style and of their doctrines, and of this whole class of proofs and subjects?

Another view is that the history of the patriarchs and judges is strictly true, but not of them as individuals; but as a history of races and revolutions. Abraham, Joseph, and Samuel are, according to this view, not the names of individuals, but ideal types of principles or of races. They are *myths*, that is, "ideas clothed in facts." And these myths were invented to explain subsequent events. Just as if the history of the beginning of the American Revolution about the stamp act and the tax on tea, and the battle of Bunker Hill, had been invented to account for the present fact that the United States is an independent nation and separate from Great Britain; and that Washington was not an individual at all, but a name invented and made to represent the embodiment of the heroic deeds of our ancestors. It is certainly a sufficient answer to such a theory to say that the ancients were as palpable individualities as we are ourselves. It is no easy matter to refine and sublimate their flesh and blood and personal actions into mere myths. Does not primeval history deal with individualities as truly as the history of our own times? The same philosophy that makes Homer or Socrates, Moses or Abraham a myth, would make all the past nothing but a myth to us, and ourselves myths to our successors. The true view is a happy deliverance from such artificial and erroneous systems. It is this: The history of Bible characters was recorded for the moral improvement of mankind, by furnishing examples of virtue and vice, the one rewarded and the other punished. In and along with this history we have an embodiment of Divine Revelation, so that the doctrines and principles revealed and the duties taught are illustrated by living examples, and the well-being of those that do well, and the ill-being of those that do evil are set forth as an encouragement to do well, and a warning to cease from evil. And the revelation contained in the Old Testament and the history and record of that revelation are all so made as to be introductory to the Gospel dispensation. Moses, the law, and the prophets prepared the way for the coming of Christ.

It follows, therefore, that if the history of Bible characters is a true biography of individuals, we shall have a full face view of men and women, as they really were. Accordingly, it is not a profile picture we have, but a true full face. Their faults are recorded as faithfully as their virtues. There is no attempt made by the sacred writers to justify or explain away every appearance of a fault in the conduct of those of whom they write, nor is there any tampering with the principles of morals, to excuse them. And if the specific purpose of the writings of Moses was to prepare the chosen people for their covenant relation to Jehovah, and through them to prepare the ancient church and the world for the coming of the long promised Messiah, still it remains true that we have a truthful record of individuals, and of divine communications made to them.

The main design of the record that we have of the patriarchs, and of the chosen people of God, was to teach mankind that it was true, that God had always in some way kept up a communication with the human race. By acts, promises, commands, and manifest tokens of the Divine presence, the great idea was *alive* in the mind of some one, who in that particular, was a representative and depositary for his race, that God was still accessible to his creatures— that he was manifesting, and would still more clearly manifest, himself to mankind. First he called Abraham, then the promise was to his descendants, and in process of time they became a great people, and to them were committed the oracles of God. As mankind multiplied and spread abroad, the line became more distinctive; but as the time drew near, clearer and clearer intimations were given of the extension of the blessings of Abraham's covenant seed by the coming and kingdom of the great Messiah. Of necessity therefore the history of the chosen people who were the depositary of the divine oracles must be a record of gracious and providential interpositions, as well as of individual verities. We should expect *a priori* to find in it a supernatural element, prophecy and miracle, theophanies or divine appearances in human form, as well as a record of the accidents of humanity in communion with the Deity. Now it would be unnatural if there had been no imperfections to record in the lives of the patriarchs, judges, prophets, and kings of Israel. And if they had not been men of like passions with ourselves, or even worse, there had been no such display of sovereignty in selecting them, as would correct their pride. The intrinsic weakness of the vessel is clearly shown, that it may be confessed that it was an act of pure sovereignty that chose them as the channels of divine grace. Oftentimes their own views and cherished wishes were thwarted. Abraham's hopes in Ishmael, Isaac's in Joseph were disappointed. The promised seed came not in the line of either. The prophetic prëeminence was lodged elsewhere. The patriarchs received special divine favours, not because they were perfect—not because they were better than all the rest of their cotemporaries. It may be doubted, speaking after the manner of men, if Melchisedek was not more entitled to the distinction of being the progenitor of the chosen race than Abram of the Chaldees.

At least, as it was not a reward for extraordinary piety that the patriarchs received such favours, so neither was it because of their transgressions, but in spite of them. It was not for their sakes, but for a far higher and greater purpose. And as a corrective of corruption and pride—of despondency and presumption, a faithful narrative has been given of them as men, and the Divine sovereignty is manifested in their salvation, and in the manner of their treatment, as well as in the record that has been made of the revelation made to them. It was certainly a palpable lesson to the Hebrew and a powerful corrective of his pride, to know that, if through David's race, he was of Abraham, "the friend of God," Ishmael was not less Abraham's son, and Esau was Jacob's brother, and Moab and Ammon were the sons of Lot. The Bible is a map that traces all nations to a common origin, and shows that though their lines of descent are continually crossing one another, still God has kept his chosen people distinct, that in them he might show forth his sovereignty, and the severity of his judgments, and the greatness of his mercy.

It is not necessary for maintaining this design of Bible biography, that we should deny that there were any other purposes in view. Collateral and minor ends were no doubt answered in the Pentateuch, and in the history of the Judges, and through the whole and by the whole, the ancient church is seen as a type of that which was to come.

While, then, it is a painful fact, it is nevertheless an instructive one, that we have no perfect biography in the Bible, except that of the Son of God, the Holy One. The patriarchs were all guilty of some dark sin. The apostles were not blameless. They all had their failings. We must remember, however, that the Bible in recording the sins of patriarchs and apostles does not approve of their sinful acts. The Bible does not tell us that such acts were the perfect fruits of their faith. On the contrary, their creed condemned every one of their sins. Their errors were not the consequences of their religion, but in spite of it. It was not because they were pious, that they fell into such grievous sins, but because they had not piety enough to resist their own depraved inclinations and the devil's temptations. And in the fact that the sacred writers describe with impartiality both the faults and the virtues of the founders of their nation, we have a strong proof that they wrote by the inspiration of God. As Jews they were exceedingly proud, and disposed to magnify everything that belonged to their nation. It must have been therefore sorely against their natural feelings to record the glaring misdeeds of their fathers, patriarchs, judges, and prophets. It was against their national pride and patriotism, to do so; yet we find them all honest, faithful, and impartial in their memoirs of the heroes of their nation. Even Morell, in his Philosophy of Religion, admits that if the Spirit of God was in the Hebrew church, "then the writings which embody this religious state are inspired." But in the record of their religious state we are not to expect "a higher religion or a more perfect morality than actually existed in those times; hence accordingly the imperfections both in moral and religious ideas which are mixed up with all their sacred writings."—Page 169.

Finally. It is not true therefore that the Old Testament is a failure. It accomplished all it was intended to do. It is not true that the Creator set up one religion for one race in the age of the patriarchs, and finding that it did not work well, tried to mend it by the Mosaic dispensation, and then repaired Moses's institutes by the prophets. This is the mere garrulity of obsolete Deism. The religion of the Bible is one. Christianity is as old as the creation. Abel and Noah were christians as much as Peter and Paul. They looked forward, while Peter and Paul looked back. They anticipated the sacrifice on Calvary, while the apostles and all christians since the incarnation keep it in remembrance. God's plan of revealing redemption from the beginning was to be progressive to the incarnation. The old dispensation was not intended to be effectual or final in itself. It was the shadow of good things to come. And the promises fulfilled in us are as necessary as the promises given to the patriarchs. "They are like the two parts of a tally. The fathers had one part in the promises, and we the other in the fulfilment, and neither would have been complete without the other."—Barnes.

## CHAPTER IV.

### SAMSON'S PARENTS—THE HERO PROMISED.

"Oh, wherefore was my birth from heaven foretold
Twice by an angel?———
Why was my breeding ordered and prescribed
As of a person separate to God,
Designed for great exploits?"—*Samson.*

In a previous chapter I have considered at some length the plan, method, and design of the biographies of the Scriptures, especially of the earlier ones, and have attempted to set forth briefly the true nature of the revelation and inspiration of the Bible, which not only contains the word of God, but is the word of God itself. This has been deemed a necessary introduction to the inspired history which it is our purpose now to explain, because confessedly in our day, the question is, What does the Bible reveal? As a book, as the book, and as a volume of history it has its place in the world, from which its enemies have despaired of ever being able to remove it. The great question therefore now is, What does the Bible say?—Can we arrive at a reliable interpretation of the Scriptures? Most certainly. We have a revelation from God, and an inspired record of that revelation. And this revelation and record are both made in such a way that we may know the will of God for our salvation. As we believe with Bishop Horsley that every word of the Bible is from God, and every man is interested in it, so it is our purpose, in these chapters, to give a condensed commentary upon the text, and draw from it the life of our hero. We shall introduce to you therefore, without further ceremony, Samson's parents receiving the promise of the hero-child.

What then was their political condition, and how were they circumstanced as to their neighbours?

"And the children of Israel did evil again." That is, according to the Hebrew, "added to commit evil," the evil of the idolatry of the surrounding heathen, which in their case was both treason and impiety. "And the Lord delivered them into the hand of the Philistines forty years."

Here are three points to be noticed.

1. Who were the Philistines?

2. In what sense did their oppression of Israel continue forty years?

3. What is the meaning of the phrase, "And the Lord delivered them into the hand of the Philistines?"

First. The Philistines are believed to have been a colony from Egypt. The old name *Palestina* is supposed to be a corruption of *Philistia*. If so, the whole land of promise derived one of the names by which it is designated from a people who never possessed more than a small part of it. The name *Palestina* was first applied to the strip of country lying along the Mediterranean from Lydda to Gaza; then to that part of Canaan between the sea and the Jordan, and finally to the whole country; so that the land of promise, Judea, Canaan, and Palestine became synonymous.

It is evident that the Philistines in the days of the judges, and probably in the days of the patriarchs also, were superior to any of their neighbours. They were certainly a powerful people in Abraham's day. This we should expect, if they were an Egyptian colony, for the ancient Egyptians were altogether the most civilized and the best people of their day. Some suppose the Philistines were the Arabians expelled from Egypt, and known as "the Shepherd Kings," on account of whose depredations on Egypt, every shepherd was reckoned "an abomination." As a proof of their superiority, we may observe that it is said in 1 Samuel xiii. 19–21, that in the beginning of Saul's reign no smith was found in Israel, so that the Israelites were obliged to go down to the land of the Philistines to sharpen their ploughshares, coulters, axes, and mattocks.

Even after David's conquest, we read of the Philistines as a powerful people. They rose in rebellion against Jehoram, and made great slaughter in the land of Judah during the reign of Ahab. They were again brought into subjection by Hezekiah. The prophets Isaiah, Amos, Zephaniah, Jeremiah, and Ezekiel allude to them. They were partially subdued by Esarhaddon, king of Assyria, and afterwards by the king of Egypt, and still more reduced by Nebuchadnezzar, king of Babylon. The Persians, and then the Greeks under Alexander the Great, overran their country. Some allusion is made to them in the days of the Asmonean Princes, and then they are lost from history.

From Amos ix. 7, and Jeremiah xlvii. 4, learned men think that the Caphtorim were descendants of Mizraim, father of the Egyptians. Gen. x. 13, 14. And from Deut. ii. 23, it appears, the Caphtorim drove out the Avim from Hazerim to Azzah, (that is, Gaza,) and dwelt in their stead. If, as it seems to us, the Casluhim, Caphtorim, Cherethites, and Philistines are one and the same people, then we should conclude that the Philistines were from Egypt, and that the most influential part of them came to the main land of Syria from Crete. As the Cherethites and the Cretans are the same, are we not authorized to identify Caphtor and Crete? See Ezekiel xxv. 16; Zeph. ii. 5; 1 Samuel xxx. 14, 15. From the history of the kings of Judah, it appears that their guards were sometimes Philistines, who were known under the name of Pelethites and Cherethites. These Pelethite (Philistine) guards answered to the Capigis among the Turks. If Caphtor is not Crete, where is it? If the Philistines were not from Egypt, whence came they? Does not their history render their Egyptian origin very probable? Some, indeed, think that Caphtor was in the Delta. Dr. Clark believes it identical with Cyprus, but gives no satisfactory reason. If, as some think, Casluhim meant inhabitants of Colchis, then they were of Egyptian origin; for almost all authors agree that Colchis was peopled from Egypt. "And Pathrusim, and Casluhim, out of whom came Philistim and Caphtorim." Gen. x. 14.

The government of the Philistines was spasmodic and changeable. In the time of David and in the days of Abraham, they had a king; but during the administration of the Judges, they had a government very similar to that of the Hebrews. Their five great cities constituted so many states, each having its own chief. These chiefs are in our text called lords. The term, *seranim*, is found only in the plural. Sometimes, however, they are found confederate together, making common cause against their national enemy. They were essentially one people. They had the same laws and religion, and spoke the same language.

Secondly. It is probable the forty years date from the ascendency of their enemies as recorded, Judges x. 6—8; that is, from Eglon to Samson, including the twenty years of his administration. The case seems to stand in this way: the Philistines, who were the most powerful of all their enemies at that time, had tyrannized over the Israelites for twenty years, when Samson appeared as their deliverer. During this twenty years, they had suffered oppression without any redress, or any one to deliver them. Samson arose and acted as their champion for twenty years, which make the forty years of the text. It must be confessed, however, that the chronology and dates of this period are not very clearly stated. The connection of the text is with the period occupied in the previous chapters. In the beginning of this thirteenth chapter, the writer seems to turn back, and speak again of the previous oppressions of his countrymen by the Philistines, in order to introduce Samson as their champion. And hence, he says, that from the beginning of this particular ascendency of the Philistines to the death of Samson, when he finished his deliverance, for the Hebrews, it was forty years.

Thirdly. After Shamgar's exploits as recorded in a previous chapter, the Hebrews had a little repose. But now as they have again departed from the living God, so the Philistines are again commissioned to punish them. "The Lord delivered them into the hand of the Philistines." The struggle between the Hebrews and Philistines was one of great obstinacy and vicissitude. It was a border war. Neither was able wholly to subdue the other.

In the second chapter, fourteenth verse, the enemies of God's chosen people are called "spoilers;" that is, robbers, such as were plundering the Canaanites. The term also means, oppressors in general. And to them it is said, "the Lord sold the Israelites." The Hebrew for *sold* signifies "to alienate the possession of anything for a valuable consideration." It is sometimes used, however, without the annexed idea of an equivalent rendered. When, therefore, as in this passage, it is said, "the anger of the Lord was hot against Israel, and he sold them into the hands of their enemies around about them," the meaning is not that the Lord made the Israelites to sin, but that he withdrew from them his peculiar protection, and that he did this because of their rebellion against him. The scriptures often represent the withdrawing of God's favour as the greatest calamity that can befall a nation or an individual. See Psa. xliv. 13; Isa.

l. 1; Deut. xxxii. 30; and Judges iii. 8; and iv. 8. Moses had told them that, when they were disobedient to the Lord, he would withdraw from them his peculiar presence, which was their only safety. The delivery of the Hebrews, therefore, into the hands of the Philistines, was nothing but the fulfilment of the solemn threatening made to their fathers and repeated to themselves. It was but the execution of the just sentence of God, who was then their king, for their disobedience. And to secure this execution, it was only necessary for the divine protection to be withdrawn. When left to themselves they were an easy prey to the warlike heathen. The absence of the sun leaves us in darkness. God is not the author of sin, nor can men blame their Creator with their evil ways. Learned theologians have recourse to various intermediate explanations by which to reconcile divine sovereignty and man's free agency. But it is quite sufficient for me to know that God is sovereign and man is free. And though I were not able to perceive how God "sold" the Israelites into the hand of the Philistines, and that yet it was for their own sins, or how Pharaoh hardened his own heart, and that God hardened Pharaoh's heart; yet still, I am persuaded of both facts, and hold them both to be consistent with ethical and mental philosophy. What if there be a transcendental difficulty in such a harmony? Is there not just the same in every question that is any how connected with the origin of moral or physical evil? It is doubtless true that God is sometimes represented in the Bible as doing what he only permits. And yet I am frank to say that I feel no necessity for, nor do I take pleasure in dwelling on such theological distinctions. I see not that these distinctions between a divine permission and a divine appointment, founded on the *vis inertiæ* of created minds, which are as clay in the hands of the potter, are really any relief. These metaphysical distinctions do not relieve human accountability from the difficulties that mental philosophy or the light of nature throws upon it. The only explanation of the difficulty is the authority of God for the facts. Nor am I able to find such distinctions in the word of God. Where do the scriptures qualify, or attempt to explain and harmonize the statements about Pharaoh's heart? Why should our theologians be more jealous of the divine character than the writers of the Bible? Where is our faith? Is not God just, and is he not sovereign? May we not rest satisfied with the facts stated by inspired men upon the authority of God?

Is it not true, every Lord's day, that some of you listen to the divine word, and that hearing it with indifference, or with aversion, you refuse obedience, and thereby harden your own heart under the very process that was graciously designed to soften it? And in doing so, are you not still conscious of your own free agency? The offer of pardon is made to you in good faith. There is no deficiency in it. The sun that melts one substance hardens another; not because the sun is in any respect another and a different body to the one from what it is to the other. The ground of the different and diverse effect is in the nature of the body acted upon by the sun, and not owing to any change or defect in the orb of day. Salvation is always of the Lord, and perdition is always the work of the sinner's own hand. There is nothing between the greatest sinner and salvation, but his own unwillingness to accept of it as a free, sovereign gift through Jesus Christ as the only Redeemer.

St. Augustine explains this *crux criticorum*, by saying, "God does not harden men by infusing malice into them, but by not imparting mercy to them. God does not work this hardening of heart in man, but he is said to harden him whom he will not soften, to blind him whom he will not enlighten, and to repel him whom he will not call."*

From the second verse, we learn that Samson's father belonged to the tribe of Dan, and the town of Zorah, which seems to have been a border town between the territories of Dan and Judah, and near the country of the Philistines. Joshua xv. 33. Eusebius says Zorah was ten miles from Eleutheropolis. Calmet thinks the Zorites of 1 Chron. ii. 54, and the Zorathites of 1 Chron. iv. 2, belonged to Manoah's town.

"Barren and bare not" is the usual Hebrew affirmation emphatic—"Thou shalt die and not live." "And he confessed and denied not." "But Sarai was barren: she had no child."

All we know of Manoah impresses us with the belief, that Josephus is correct in saying that he was a man of great virtue, had but few equals, and was without dispute the principal person of his country in his day. His wife's name is not recorded in the Bible, nor by Josephus. He says, however, that she was celebrated for her beauty and her piety.

Samson's father was a man of extraordinary faith. He is the only one of whom the Bible speaks, that received a promise from an angel or prophet without hesitation or doubt. Abraham required some proof. Sarah "laughed." The Shunamite woman said to Elisha, "Nay my Lord, do not lie unto thine handmaid." Zachariah said, "Whereby shall I know this?" and was struck dumb for his unbelief until John the Baptist was born. And Mary, the mother

* Non obdurat Deus impartiendo malitiam, sed non impartiendo misericordiam. Non operatur Deus in homine ipsam duritiam cordis, sed indurare eum dicitur quem mollire noluerit, sic etiam excœcare quem illuminare noluerit, et repellere eum quem noluerit vocare.—Epis. 194, ad Sixtum.

of our Lord, said, "How can this thing be?" But when Manoah is told by his wife and then by the angel what is to take place, he believed without any hesitation, and only desired to be instructed as to how they were to bring up the promised child. "And the angel of the Lord appeared unto the woman, and said unto her, Behold now, thou art barren, and bearest not: but thou shalt conceive, and bear a son. Now therefore, beware, I pray thee, and drink not wine, nor strong drink, and eat not any unclean thing. For, lo, thou shalt conceive, and bear a son: and no razor shall come on his head; for the child shall be a Nazarite unto God from the womb; and he shall begin to deliver Israel out of the hand of the Philistines."—Verses 3–5.

"And the angel of the Lord," that is, "the Son of God himself," according to Diodati and most evangelical commentators. Of this matter we shall speak again in the next chapter.

The angel told the woman what she already well knew—what was indeed the cause of great grief to her—not to upbraid her or aggravate her grief. There is no reproach cast upon her in the angel's address. His purpose was to give her confidence—to convince her that he was a true prophet, and competent to make the promise of a son—and that she ought therefore to believe his words. Like a skilful medical man, he describes first the disease, that he may inspire his patient with confidence in his sympathy, and ability to apply the proper remedy. Our blessed Lord followed the same method in arresting the attention of the impotent man at the pool. He awakened him to the fact of his presence, and assured him of his sympathy, and inspired him with hope by asking him if he would be made whole. And he told the woman of Samaria enough of her life to convince her he was a prophet, and prepare her at last to confess that he was the Messiah himself.

The prohibition in the fourth verse does not imply that she had been guilty of excess. Nor is it intimated that such things were not lawful at other times and to other persons. It is true some meats were regarded as unclean among the Jews. The distinction of clean and unclean animals is at least as old as Noah, and no doubt as old as sacrifices. But it was especially forbidden to a Nazarite to touch anything unclean. The angel would have her understand that the sanctifying of her child was to begin with herself. From her conception, the child was to be regarded as consecrated in an especial manner to God. And if during her gestation and nursing, she was thus abstemious, the extraordinary strength of the child would be the less liable to be ascribed to any false or fictitious cause. There was a natural fitness in the prescribed regimen and temperament to produce a healthful child, but his superhuman strength cannot be accounted for from merely natural causes. A miraculous agency was employed, as we shall see in the unfoldings of his history; yet it was then as in many other cases, the divine rule, that the ordinary natural means should be used. Miracles do not supersede, but go beyond and above ordinary agencies. There is always a harmony between divine efficiency and human agency.

"A Nazarite unto God from the womb," means one set apart and consecrated especially to the service of God. There is no connection between a Nazarite and a Nazarene. The latter means an inhabitant of Nazareth, the town of our Lord's parents. But *a Nazarite* was one wholly devoted to God. And of such it was especially required, that they should not shave their head. The law of the Nazarite can be found in Numbers vi. Though expected to be a person of uncommon self-denial and sanctity, the Nazarite was not a recluse, nor an ascetic. He did not live in a cell, nor on a pillar, nor in the wilderness. He might eat, drink, marry and live in society as other men, excepting that he was to avoid all ceremonial pollution, and especially never to come in contact with a dead body. The vow to abstain from wine, and not to shave the head, might be for a limited time or for life. In the case of Samson, of Samuel, and of John the Baptist, however, the consecration was made before their birth and was to continue till death. I believe Samson is the first person mentioned in the Bible by name as an actual Nazarite. Like Isaac, Samuel, and John the Baptist, he was the only son of a mother long childless. "Mercies long waited for, often prove signal mercies, and it is made to appear they were worth waiting for, and by them others may be encouraged to continue their hope in God's mercy."—*Henry.*

The mother of Israel's hero drinks nothing but water, and the child himself tastes nothing but nature's beverage. "And never did wine," says the pious Hall, "make so strong a champion as water did here. The power of nourishment is not in the creatures, but in their Maker. Daniel and his three companions kept their complexion with the same diet wherewith Samson got his strength; he that gave power to the grape, can give it to the stream. O God, how justly do we raise our eyes from our tables unto thee, who canst make water nourish and wine enfeeble!"

"Oh! madness to think use of strongest wines
And strongest drinks our chief support of health,
When God with these forbidden made choice to rear
His mighty champion, strong above compare,
Whose drink was only from the liquid brook."

Special holiness eminently becomes special appointments to divine service. Special care in food and drink was required of her who was to be the mother of Samson. The man of the world may take his full scope and deny himself nothing. And verily he hath his reward. He may indulge the pride of his heart and the lust of his eyes, not without sin indeed, but with less guilt than one who professes to be a christian. For having named the name of Christ, we must be careful to depart from all iniquity. If we are Christ's, we must have his spirit. If christians, we are consecrated to God as true Nazarites. The man of the world has all his good things now, and it is a miserable, poor portion. The believer's good things are to come. They are in Heaven.

"And he shall begin to deliver Israel." Samson only began to deliver Israel, for it was not till the days of David, that the Philistines were entirely subdued. "Begin to deliver" seems here to mean, some deliverance—pledges, specimens of what their God was able to do for them, and proofs that although they had been so grievously oppressed by the Amorites on their eastern border, and now by the Philistines on the west, still he had not wholly forsaken them. The deliverance begun by Samson was most timely. This was the darkest hour of their oppression. Their condition was most humiliating and their enemies most insultingly cruel. It was God's time for Moses to come, when the tale of bricks was doubled. "Begin to deliver" also suggests that God's usual method is to work gradually. He has ordered that one shall sow, and another reap. One lays the foundation, another brings forth the capstone with shoutings, crying "grace, grace, unto it."

Samson was the first hero of the tribe of Dan. Jacob in his dying blessing had said: "Dan shall be a serpent by the way, an adder in the path, biting the heels of the horse, so that his rider shall fall backwards." Gen. xlix. 16, 17. And as the name *Dan* signifies judge or judgment, it has been suggested, that it was a divine foretelling of Samson, that Jacob uttered in dying, when he said, "Dan shall judge his people." That is, of this tribe shall arise a distinguished judge. And this could be no other than Samson. The prophecy related to the fortunes and exploits of Dan's posterity, and not to himself personally, and was fulfilled more remarkably in Manoah's son, than in any other man of his tribe. As the territory of Dan bordered on the cities of the Philistines, it was natural for them to be the most exposed to their depredations. It was therefore proper that the avenger and deliverer of Israel should arise out of this tribe.

We see also that afflictions are occasions for God's appearance. Divine help is always opportunely. The promise is that grace shall be given to us not before, but according to our day. Only the sick really know the blessings of recovery to health. If Manoah's wife had not been in grief, the angel had not been sent to comfort her. It has been happily remarked that in the Bible angels and prophets were often sent with glad tidings to women that were without children, and in much sorrow on that account. And it has been asked why was this, and why were the sons thus promised so distinguished, since but few great men have sons equal to themselves? There is an answer to all the points of this inquiry without impeaching either the justice or goodness of God. The inferiority of the sons of great men may be owing to the weakness of the mother, or to the neglect of their early training. It is well known that some distinguished men have married women not at all their equals, or fit to be their companions. And it is quite as well known, that great men are so occupied with public cares, or so diligently employed in the pursuit of knowledge, that their own children are often neglected. The main point in hand here, however, is the illustration that God's gracious deliverances are always opportunely sent. I am aware that various conjectures have been made to satisfy the rather over curious, if not profane, infidel question—Why did the angel appear to the wife rather than to the husband? No reason is stated. Nor do I see that we are under any obligations to vindicate our narrative for this omission. The fact of the angel's appearance is recorded. But we do not know whether he was sent to the woman, because it was her reproach rather than her husband's that she was not fruitful; or whether it was because she was to endure the pain of parturition; or because she took the matter more to heart than her husband did. If we must find a reason, the last is most to our mind. For it is always true, that God's mercies are well-timed and properly directed. The history of the pious proves conclusively, that if Satan ply his heavy batteries upon the weakest, God does not fail to address consolation to those that are most in need. The promises of God are like a certain kind of bridge; the more heavy the pressure upon them, the stronger they are. The believer is fortified abundantly with exceeding great and precious promises. Eve was the most dejected; to her therefore was the promise especially addressed. It is not said, Adam's seed; but the seed of the woman shall bruise the serpent's head. Manoah's wife is the most troubled, to her therefore is the divine messenger sent; and sent to her: 1. Because the announcement to a barren woman of the birth of a distinguished son, would impress her and her husband and countrymen with the idea that such a son was from the Lord, and designed by him to be a special blessing. All children are divine gifts. They are God's heritage. They come only at his bidding. But when some special mission was designed, it was proper to give distinction to the appointment. 2. A son given under such solemn promises and instruction would be better taken care of. A gift thus made would be more highly valued. The education of children is a fearful responsibility. And even the best mothers need divine help and admonitions. In the East it is still considered a disgrace and a mark of divine displeasure, to have a childless house. Among the ancient Hebrews the desire for children was rendered even more intense than among other nations, because of the promises. Every Hebrew wife seems to have hoped she would be the mother of the Messiah, or at least of his progenitor. Vows and prayers and expensive ceremonies were resorted to as a means of prevailing upon God to give them children. And to this day, in the schools of the East, boys may be seen with elf locks, which are memorials of vows to God for favour granted in their gift. See verses six, seven, and eight. "Man of God," that is, a holy prophet. "Very terrible," that is, according to Diodati, "majestical, glorious and sparkling with light." The woman seems to say, his countenance was so like that of an angel of God—so commanding, so awful, and inspired me with such awe, that I feared to ask him any questions.

"Samson had not a better mother than Manoah had a wife." As a good wife, she at once told her husband of God's messenger. And Manoah at once applies at head-quarters. He goes immediately to prayer, saying, O my Lord, I pray thee, let that man of God my wife speaks of come again, and tell us fully how we are to bring up the child. He had not seen God's messenger. He has yet but a meagre account of the interview; but his faith takes hold of the promise, nothing doubting.

Josephus thinks, but without authority, that Manoah's mind was disturbed by what his wife had said of the man of God, and that he wished to have some further knowledge of this strange visitor. There is not a syllable, however, to warrant any such jealous suspicion. On the contrary, his desire was to obtain information as to the bringing up of the child. His wife in all things seems to have been dutiful, confiding, and affectionate. She reports at once, as a good wife should have done, the angelic message, to her husband—doubtless because she wished him to share in the joy of such a promise, and desired his help to keep all the admonitions given to her. She seems to have been so overjoyed at the announcement that she was to have a son, that she ran away from the man of God, hastening home from the field, without asking him how she was to bring up a child to whom so important a mission was committed.

And surely Manoah's solicitude to have more full instruction from the angel was well. For the care of children is a very great concern. Happy would it be for us as a people, if all our parents, like this pious Danite, oftener prayed: "Teach me what we shall do to the child that shall be born to us."

From Manoah and his wife let us learn the duty and privilege of dedicating our little ones to God. He has a property in us and our households that cannot be destroyed. Nor does he ever relinquish or alienate his rights to our children. It is therefore our duty to acknowledge him in our families, and to dedicate to him the children he has given us. This dedication is a solemn covenant, as well as a sacrament. In it God says to us: Take these little ones and bring them up for me, and I will give thee thy wages. And we answer, Lord, we dedicate them to thee, imploring thy blessing to rest upon them.

The care of children should begin before they are born—even before they are conceived. A celebrated physician says: "The first duty parents owe to their children is, to convey health and strength, a good constitution of body and mind to them, as far as it is in their power; by a proper care of their own health, and a conscientious abstinence from vice and excess of every kind." The ancient Romans were extremely careful as to the health and condition of mothers. If ignorance as to the effect of a mother's health and state of mind on the constitution of her child could ever be plead as an excuse for entailing a host of ailments upon her posterity, it surely cannot now be offered; for by means of the press and of public lecturing, the whole subject has been popularized—perhaps too much so. At least ignorance is no longer an excuse. And if the laws of nature on this subject are well understood in their application to the lower animals, why should they be neglected or despised in man? Health of mind and body should be a prerequisite of marriage. And the most enlightened attention should be bestowed on women during their child-bearing. This subject deserves the most serious consideration from patriots, philanthropists, and christians. The civil, intellectual, and moral well-being of our nation is and will be greatly affected by a proper regard to it. It is not a matter of doubt, or a point yet to be discussed. It is already demonstrated that many diseases, tempers, dispositions, and habits are hereditary. "Many of the ill habits of body that children bring into the world with them are owing to the irregularities of their mothers; (and of their fathers;) and most of the diseases of which so many young children die, arise from a bad mass of blood communicated to them." "Women with child ought conscientiously to avoid whatever they have reason to think will be any way prejudicial to the health or good constitution of the fruit of their life."—*Henry.*

The proper idea of educating children is to fit them for the duties of life and the realities of a fast-coming eternity. To do this they must be trained. Training combines, 1. both instruction and government. Its field is both the mind and the body. It reduces to life the precepts which are to regulate them when they are grown. To train a child properly is to form it again into the image in which man was created. It is to recover it from the ruins of the fall. This cannot be done at once. But it can be begun, and the completion will follow in heaven. To train a child requires patience, faith, courage, perseverance, and divine assistance.

2. To bring up a child in "the nurture and admonition of the Lord," instruction and example are essential. It is the nature of a child to imitate what is around it. The influence of example is as certain as the action of the air upon its body. Influences educate the child long before it is large enough to be sent from home to school. It is in the unwritten, unspoken teachings of home in our tenderest years that our destiny has its beginnings. Every word, tone, look, frown, smile, and tear, witnessed in childhood, performs its part in training the infant for eternity. Instruction should begin early, but let it be oral, and consist chiefly of a few moral precepts, Bible stories, and chaste fables. A great error in our times is the pressing of the infantile mind; cramming the memory with what the child does not understand, and at the same time so compressing and cramping it as to prevent the proper physical development, and impair the reasoning faculties. Another of the alarming evils of our day is the circulation of demoralizing publications. Earnest warning and entreaties on this subject have often fallen from this pulpit. But the warning cannot be too often repeated. The influence of immoral prints and books is calculated more than anything else to corrupt the morals, and enfeeble the intellects of the juvenile portion of our country. To circulate such publications is a serious offence against God and man; and yet I greatly fear it is a growing evil; nor do I see any corrective so available, so potential and so practicable, as family government and instruction. Let the home be for amusement, pleasure, knowledge, and religion as attractive as possible.

3. In the bringing up of children, prayer, deep, earnest, believing prayer is essential. The preservation of children

is a constant miracle. After all our solicitude and pains-taking, and watching and heart-bleeding, we have to trust them to God. We are shut up to wrestling with God, as the last resort saying, Peradventure they may live; or as Abraham himself, Oh that Ishmael might live! Parental solicitude is not only justified, but expressly enjoined in God's word. The apostle speaks of it, as a great commendation of Timothy and of his mother and grandmother, that from his infancy he had been made acquainted with the Scriptures, which were able to make him wise unto salvation through faith in Christ Jesus. "Train up a child," says Solomon, "in the way he should go, and when he is old, he will not depart from it."

He is not prepared to discharge his duties to himself, his country, and his God, as a parent, who does not see and feel that the art of education is both the most important and difficult in the world. It has been so considered by many of the greatest men that have ever lived. Many of the greatest minds and largest hearts have spent their wisdom and strength, in advancing the education of mankind in morals and religion.

By Manoah's example, we are taught where to obtain aid and direction in bringing up our children. As soon as he is informed that he is to have a son, he falls to praying that he may know how to order the child—to know what he should do unto him. Verses eight and twelve. "When I see the strength of Manoah's faith, I marvel not that he had a Samson to his son; he saw not the messenger, he heard not the errand, he examined not the circumstances; yet now he takes thought, not whether he should have a son, but how he shall order the son which he must have." —*Hall.*

It is true that we are eminently blessed with elementary school books, and the schools of our country, especially for

God, because, in spirituality and higher morals, it has been surpassed by the New Testament, is absurd. A boy's grammar was just the book he wanted when he had to learn the elements of language. And in manhood the grammar of his youth is not superfluous or lost because he embodies all the knowledge it contained, and even more. The elements of language are not superfluous to the language matured. If the promises, types, and predictions of the Old Testament be arranged, therefore, as stars, in clusters and constellations, we can readily see how one arose in Eden, and another to Enoch, and another to Noah after the flood, and another to Abraham, and another and another, till the whole heavens became luminous, when the star in the East guided the wise men to the infant Redeemer at Bethlehem.

V. We are now prepared, I trust, to say that "the angel of the Lord," the angel of Jehovah's presence, and the divine manifestations made in the Old Testament, were foreshadowings of the great Incarnation. In them the Son of God declared that his delights were with the sons of men from all eternity, and was manifesting forth his glory in such measure as was proper to keep alive the promise of his coming, when the fulness of time should arrive. And in the application of the appellation Angel of Jehovah to the Messiah, we have a proof of the divinity of our Lord Jesus Christ.

"No man hath seen God at any time; the only begotten Son, which is in the bosom of the Father, he hath declared him." "He is God manifest in the flesh."—John i. 18; 1 Tim. iii. 16.

It is not, therefore, without reason that the learned are of the opinion that this ninth verse is of peculiar construction and emphasis, meaning that it was the Lord God himself to whom Manoah prayed, who hearkened to his voice, and then appeared to him and his wife, and that he appeared to them in the person of his Son, veiled as an angel.

VI. In all the varieties of manner in which, in times past, God spake unto the fathers, the Logos, the Word, of John i., was the Revealer. This is emphatically true of the revelations made by the Angel-Jehovah. In the revelation of the divine will "by facts, by words," and by appearances, or visible forms of the divine glory, of which record is made in the Old Testament, there is a constant reference to the Author of Creation, implying by such a reference the right and power to make all such revelations; but the most remarkable manifestation of the Logos, "the Word," in the Old Testament, if I am not greatly mistaken, is this of the Angel-Jehovah.

This is the mysterious personage who appeared to Abraham, "the friend of God," who rejoiced in seeing Messiah's day. And in the various passages of scripture in which the appearance of the Angel of Jehovah is described, we find him using the first person, and speaking, and acting, and receiving homage and worship, not as a distinct person from, but as the manifestation or visible operation of the Godhead. The Angel of the Lord, then, is to be understood as Jehovah-Jesus in his visibility. And in this manifestation of Jesus Christ in the Theophanies of the Old Testament, we have, in some degree, an explanation of how he came to be "the desire of all nations;" for it is well known that heathen nations of old, both savage and civilized, had some notion of the incarnation of their gods, and of the necessity of such incarnation.

If we are not mistaken, Messiah Jesus is expressly called an Angel, the Angel of the Lord, in the Old Testament, and plainly so represented in the New. In addition to the texts which represent the Logos as the Revealer of God, there are some that speak of the same personage as an An-young children and the acquirement of a practical education, are not surpassed by those of any other nation. But it deserves to be always kept in mind, that in educating there is no book that can take the place of the word of God, and no means that can be made a substitute for prayer. It is the great business of a parent to secure a sound mind in a sound body for his child, and then to baptize him day by day with heavenly influences in answer to prayer. And surely it is of such children we may hope, as patriots and as followers of Christ, that they will be deliverers of Israel. The age of miracles is past. We have no right to expect angels to tell us what to do unto our children. We have a more sure word of prophecy (instruction.) The divine word is ever speaking to us, saying, "This is the way, walk ye in it." Conscience, enlightened by the divine word and spirit, is also constantly teaching us the way in which we should go. The Bible direction is to acknowledge God in all our ways, and he will direct our steps. Manoah's mind was aroused by his wife's tidings; and his faith was at once strong; and being all the more encouraged by the favours already given, he prayed to God to teach him more fully what he was to do. And though secret things belong to God, revealed things belong to us and to our children. And whenever the soul bows down before the Father of spirits, earnestly seeking to know his will, in some way or other, he will teach us his paths, Psalm xxv. 8.

"Thus at the flaming forge of life
Our fortunes must be wrought,
Thus on its sounding anvil shaped
Each burning deed and thought."

# CHAPTER V.

## JESUS CHRIST IN THE THEOPHANIES OF THE OLD TESTAMENT.

"——— Appeared before mine eyes
A man of God: his habit and his guise
Were such as holy prophets used to wear;
But in his dreadful looks there did appear
Something that made me tremble; in his eye
Mildness was mixt with awful majesty."

*Quarles' Samson.*

Testamentum Vetus de Christo exhibendo, Novum de Christo exhibito agit: Novum in veteri latet, Vetus in novo patet.—*Augustine.*

"Scriptura omnis in duo Testamenta divisa est * * Judæi Veteri utuntur, nos Novo: sed tamen diversa non sunt, quia Novum Veteris adimpletio est, et in utroque idem Testator est Christus."

*Lactantius, Div. Inst.* iv. 20.

In Judges xiii. 8—21, we have a more detailed account of the appearance of the angel of the Lord, than is to be found in any other part of the Bible. For this reason, as well as on account of the great intrinsic merit of the subject, the narrative of Samson is suspended till the next chapter.

"Angel" is rather a term of office than of nature. This term is used in the Bible to denote a messenger both human and spiritual, and also impersonal agents, as winds, fires, remarkable dispensations, &c. It seems to denote any vehicle or medium by which the Creator made known his presence or executed his will. There are evil as well as good angels, and sometimes it is thought, "angel of the Lord" means a personification of divine judgments. (See Bush's notes on Gen. xvi. 7; xxiv. 7; and Ex. iii. 2.) The most frequent application of this term is undoubtedly to the special manifestation of the Lord to the patriarchs and prophets. The Shekinah is called the angel of the Lord. Ex. xiv. 19. But in all such visible symbols of the divine glory, Jehovah himself, the God of Abraham, Isaac, and Jacob, the very same that appeared in the bush, and by whose good will Joseph was preserved, is to be considered as present. "The angel of the Lord" is literally the Angel-Jehovah, or Jehovah, the Sent One, and is none other than God manifest, the Lord Jesus Christ. In the Bible, God the Father is never spoken of as *sent*, but the Messiah is so represented in the Old Testament, and Christ is so spoken of in the New Testament, and actually claims himself to have come from and to be sent by the Father. In finding therefore that the angel of the Lord is Jehovah, God, the Lord himself, we shall establish our proposition, that in the Theophanies of the Old Testament we have Jesus Christ manifested as God.

"And the angel of the Lord came again," v. 9. This is the same angel that appeared first to the woman, and the same that appeared to Abraham, Lot, Moses, Joshua, Gideon, and others, and is the Messiah-Christ. In the eighteenth verse, "the angel of the Lord said unto him, Why askest thou thus after my name, seeing it is secret?" Here the Hebrew word for *secret* is the same that Isaiah uses for wonderful. Isa. ix. 6. "And his name shall be called wonderful." Hence it is concluded, that the true meaning of the clause, "seeing it is secret," is, it is wonderful. The angel then means to say that, his name Wonderful, signified that he was the promised Messiah.

In Genesis xxii. 11, the same appellation is used. "And

the angel of the Lord called unto him out of heaven, and said, Abraham, Abraham," and yet in the first verse of the same chapter it is said that it was God who tempted Abraham, and commanded him to sacrifice his son. See also verses fourteen, fifteen, sixteen, which clearly identify the angel of Jehovah and God as one and the same. And in Gen. xxiv. 7, the angel of the Lord is identified with God himself. The same thing is clear from Ex. iii. 2, 6, 10, 14; Numb. xx. 22; Judges ii. 5; and vi. 11–40; 2 Samuel xxiv. 16; 2 Kings xix. 35; 1 Chron. xxi. 12.

Now these Scriptures taken together prove, 1. That Hagar, Abraham, and Moses, believed God to be invisible, and yet that they had certain direct communications from him. There was either a shape, or voice, or both, or some representation of God made to them visibly—some divine manifestation that came in some way within the reach of their senses; and this representation was called the "angel of Jehovah," "the angel of his presence," and was identified with Jehovah himself—received the worship, and acknowledged the attributes, and performed the same works which the Scriptures ascribe to God.

The invisibility as well as the spirituality of the Supreme Being is explicitly taught in the Bible—in both the Old and the New Testaments. See Ex. xxxiii. 20; Job ix. 11; John i. 18; and verse thirty-seven; Rev. i. 20; Col. i. 15; Heb. xi. 27; 1 Tim. vi. 16. And yet according to numerous texts of Scripture, God has been pleased, at various times and in different places, to put himself in communication with mankind. He has caused his voice to be heard and his shape to be seen. In Gen. xvi. 7, we have the first distinct divine manifestation revealed by name. Here the epithet is the one so often used in the Old Testament—"angel of the Lord." And it is evident from the text that Hagar understood the angel of Jehovah to be Jehovah himself; for she called the name of the Jehovah that spake unto her, "thou God of visibility."* These manifestations of God were made in a way suitable to the senses and capacities of man. The divine glory was of necessity veiled. And hence the manifestation was called "the angel of God's presence," that is, his messenger. So much of Godhead was manifested as the creature could bear. And by this method of revealing himself, it pleased God to keep open a communication with our race, until the fulness of time came, when he actually manifested himself in the flesh. By these divine appearances the faith of mankind was kept alive, that in due time the promise should be fulfilled, and the Word should become flesh, and the Seed of the woman bruise the serpent's head.

2. The appellation "angel of the Lord," therefore, in the Old Testament is to be understood as meaning the Messiah. Such divine appearances were manifestly pledges of God's continued good will to men. They were evidences of his repeated gracious interpositions. They were types of the coming incarnation. In the form of "a man of God," or of an angel, it was Jesus Christ, that appeared to the patriarchs, as a pledge of his future coming into the world as the long promised Messiah. The angel that redeemed Jacob from all evil, he represents as identical with the God before whom his fathers had walked, and who had fed him all his life long. And he also makes his vows to this angel as the God of Bethel, and the same who spoke to him in Padan-aram. And Hosea, speaking of this angel of Jacob, identifies him with Jehovah. See Gen. xlviii. 15, 16; and xxxi. 11–13. Jacob's language is remarkable: "The angel

* Boothroyd, Le Clerc, Houbigant, Michaelis, says this is the true reading of the passage. In their opinion also, the name of the well is "the well of the invisible God." The Targum of Jonathan, the Greek, Arabic, Chaldee, and Syriac have it thus.

which redeemed me from all evil," by which he does not mean a creature,—does not mean another and a different being from the God of his fathers, but an expletive of the name God. Is it scriptural usage then for God to be called by the name, Angel? In Jacob's earlier life, we have an instance. He wrestled with an angel at the ford Jabbok till the breaking of day, and yet he says, speaking of this angel at Peniel, "I have seen God face to face." In the divine revelation to Abraham of the doom of the cities of the plain, Jehovah himself, or God the Son, is clearly to be recognized in one of the angels. In the third chapter of Exodus, we have one of the most illustrious recorded appearances of the angel of the Lord to be found in the Bible. Here the angel of the Lord, and God, and Jehovah are interchangeable. In the second verse he who is called the angel of the Lord (Jehovah) appears in the bush, and in the fourth verse he is called Lord (Jehovah) and God. And in the sixth verse, the same Angel-Jehovah who appears in the bush and is called Lord and God, speaking of himself says: "I am the God of thy father, the God of Abraham, the God of Isaac, and the God of Jacob. And Moses hid his face; for he was afraid to look upon God." And in verses eleven and twelve, Moses said unto God, addressing the angel of the Lord, of the first verse, who was in the bush, and in the fourteenth verse—"God said unto Moses, I am that I am; and he said, Thus shalt thou say unto the children of Israel, I AM hath sent me unto you." And in the next verse he repeats that he is the Lord God of their fathers, the God of Abraham, Isaac, and Jacob. Throughout the whole narrative and dialogue of Moses' call and inauguration into office as deliverer of Israel, the angel of the Lord is Jehovah, and in this appearance of the Lord God, we recognize no other personage than the angel of the Covenant, the angel of Jehovah's presence, who is Messiah-

Christ. The Angel-Jehovah, who dwelt in the glory-cloud, and who pledged himself to conduct the Hebrews to the land of promise, the apostle tells us expressly was Christ. 1 Cor. x. 9. We have seen that the angel professes in the eighteenth verse that his name is the same that we find Isaiah applying to the Messiah in ix. 6. And again in Isa. xlii. 19, the same term—angel—that is used in the text is given to the Messiah, who is also called the Angel of the Covenant. See Mal. iii. 1; Matt. xii. 18–21. Compare also Isa. lx. 1; Heb. ii. 14; and Isa. xl. 3.

There is a gradual development of truth as taught in the Bible. The existence of God is assumed His unity and spirituality are then taught. His invisibility and yet palpable manifestations are asserted. Repeated proofs are given that Jehovah was not the mere tutelar God of the Hebrews. This was one of the great truths demonstrated by the awful controversy between Moses and Pharaoh, which was indeed a conflict between Jehovah's prime minister and the gods of Egypt. No intelligent and attentive reader of the Bible can fail to discern that a distinction is made between Jehovah as invisible, and Jehovah as manifested to men. In many parts of the Old Testament we find an exalted being, introduced as "the angel, servant, or messenger of Jehovah," who speaks of himself as distinct from the invisible and eternal Jehovah, and yet assumes to himself the honours, attributes, and works of Jehovah, and suffers himself to be addressed as God. Now how are we to understand these passages in which "the angel of God" is thus introduced?

The true interpretation of the phrase, "angel of the Lord," and the only one that reconciles all the passages in which it occurs and the allusions made to it in the Bible, is this, namely: that the angel of Jehovah in the Old Testament is Jesus Christ, who as Jehovah's servant, messenger, or angel, was manifested before the incarnation, as a proof that his heart was on his great work of redeeming man, by becoming a man, and a pledge that he would come in the fulness of time, and be actually born of a woman, made under the law, to redeem them that were under the law. (Gal. iv. 4.) The angel of the Lord then in the Theophanies of the Old Testament was the Messiah sent from God, who was the word that was God, but became flesh and dwelt among us, full of grace and truth.

From heaven he came, of heaven he spoke,
Dark clouds of gloomy night he broke,
Unveiling an immortal day.

That our views may be the more clearly understood, we repeat and sum up what we believe the Bible teaches on this subject.

I. There is one, only living and true God. This one supreme and only living and true God is alike and equally the God of the New Testament and of the Old Testament. The religion of the two great divisions of the Bible is one religion. The Bible is not a heterogeneous or contradictory mass of old or obsolete writings, but a harmonious and organized whole, each part perfect in its place and of its kind.

II. The only living and true "God is a Spirit, infinite, eternal, unchangeable, invisible." He has condescended, however, in times past to speak to the fathers by the prophets, and by his Son Jesus Christ, and his apostles. He made known his will to the patriarchs, prophets, and apostles, by his Spirit, operating directly on their minds, by dreams, visions, voices, ecstasies, symbolic acts, appearances, or manifestations in the form of an angel, or by some representation of his glory, which is called in the Old Testament, the Shekinah.

III. The leading idea of the revelation of God in the Old Testament was, the coming of the Messiah. Other great truths are taught or illustrated, but they are all in order to prepare the way for the fulfilment of this promise. And the substance of the New Testament is a record of Messiah's coming, and therein of the fulfilment of the Old Testament Scriptures.

The great design, therefore, of the Old Testament has been accomplished. The Hebrew dispensation, with the divine oracles, prepared mankind, both negatively and positively, for the appearance of the Messiah, the world-redeeming God. The purpose of divine revelation is stated in the first promise in the garden of Eden, and is prosecuted through the whole of the old dispensation. The testimony of Jesus is the bond of union, and centre in which all the Old Testament harmonizes. Without this purpose in view the Old Testament is but a loose, scattered, and badly arranged heap of poetry, history, morals, and memoirs. But with such a purpose revealed, and running through all its history, we can understand how it teaches, typifies, promises, and predicts a great salvation through the ineffable incarnation.

The whole scope and end of prophecy was the testimony of JESUS. The entire history of God's revelation in Old Testament times, is nothing but an utterance prophetic of a coming Messiah. "And upon that revelation of facts, and prediction by facts, is grounded that series of predictions by words, which God has been pleased to communicate in a supernatural manner, by his special agents."* "In the historical, the didactic, the prophetical portions of the New Testament, we discern the Old Testament, the old law, living again, in a new and spiritual life; not embalmed and laid

* Lee on Inspiration.

with reverential care aside in the grave, but arisen from the dead, and alive for evermore, like its own divine Founder."

Stephen and John, and the saints in glory are then with Moses and Elias, as the apostles were with them on the mount of transfiguration. They all sing alike the song of Moses, the servant of God, and the song of the Lamb.—Rev. xv. 3.

The Bible, as a history, testifies of Jesus. And the two great divisions of the Bible, the Old and New Testaments, are indissolubly connected, and of co-equal authority. JESUS CHRIST is the central point to which all the rays of revelation converge, and from which they again flow by the ministrations of his own Eternal Spirit.

An able author of one of the Hulsean lectures, speaking of the past development of the Scriptures, holds the following beautiful language: "This treasure of divine truth, once given, has only gradually revealed itself; how the history of the church, the difficulties, the trials, the struggles, the temptations in which it has been involved, have interpreted to it its own records. * * * Now there was much written for it there as with sympathetic ink, invisible for a season, yet ready to flash out in lines and characters of light, whenever the appointed day and hour had arrived; so that in this way the Scripture has been to the church as their garments to the children of Israel, which, during all the years of their pilgrimage in the desert, waxed not old; yea, according to rabbinical tradition, kept pace and measure with their bodies, growing with their growth, fitting the man as they had fitted the child, and this, until the forty years of their sojourn in the wilderness had expired. Or to use another comparison, which may serve to illustrate our meaning: Holy Scripture, thus progressively unfolding what it contains, might be likened fitly to some magnificent landscape, on which the sun is gradually rising, and ever as it rises is bringing out one headland into light and prominence, and then another; anon, kindling the glory-smitten summit of some far mountain, and presently lighting up the recesses of some near valley which had hitherto abided in gloom; and so, travelling on, till nothing remains in shadow, no crook nor corner hid from the light and heat of it, but the whole prospect stands out in the clearness and splendour of the highest noon.

"The true idea of scriptural development is this, that the church, informed and quickened by the Spirit of God, more and more discovers what in Holy Scripture is given her; but it is not thus that she unfolds by an independent power anything further therefrom. She has always possessed what she now possesses of doctrine and truth, only not always with the same distinctness of consciousness. She has not added to her wealth, but she has become more and more aware of that wealth; her dowry has remained always the same, but that dowry was so rich, and so rare, that only little by little she has counted over and taken stock and inventory of her jewels. She has consolidated her doctrine, compelled thereto by the provocation of her enemies, or induced to it by the growing sense of her needs. She has brought together utterances in Holy Writ, and those which, apart, were comparatively barren, when thus married—when each had thus found its complement in the other—have been fruitful to her. Those which, apart, meant little to her, have been seen to mean much when thus brought together, and read each by the light of the other. In these senses she has enlarged her dominion, her dominion having become larger to her."*

IV. It is not true, then, that the Almighty has allowed any of his dispensations to prove a failure. It is not true

---

* See Trench's Hulsean Lecture for 1853.

that the religion of Eden proving a failure, another and a new one was tried; and then, when the patriarchal faith failed, the Creator again tried to meet the wants of our race, by patching up the patriarchal religion with that of Moses; and was again obliged to add the teachings of the prophets; and, finally, becoming tired of the old religion altogether, he superseded it by introducing christianity. This is as false as it is blasphemous. There is a perfect harmony throughout the Bible. Augustin has well said, "Deus opera mutat, nec mutat consilium." (Conf. i. 4.) In all the various modes used for communicating the divine will, we find but one and the same religion—the Pentateuch, the Prophets, the Psalms, the Gospels, and the Epistles are given to us by one and the same Spirit of inspiration. The revelation is from God, and the record of that revelation is by the inspiration of the Holy Spirit. The Bible not only contains the word of God, but the Bible is the word of God, who is our Maker and final Judge.

Though the writers of the Bible are scattered over more than twenty centuries, its several books are but different members of one organized whole, and each member is perfectly adapted to the great purpose of the divine Author, and pointing all the time to him as the God and Father of our Lord Jesus Christ, through whom we have received the atonement.

It certainly cannot follow because, as Bretschneider states, and truly, that the doctrines of God and morality are far more perfectly taught in the New Testament, by Jesus Christ and his Apostles, than in the Old Testament, that, therefore, the Old Testament is obsolete. This were to say that the lad were lost in the man. The morning and the evening are but one day. But the morning twilight is in order to the noon-day splendour. To say that the Old Testament is superfluous, and of no authority, in the church of

gel, *the* Angel. The promise to Moses was, that on the withdrawal of the Lord himself, as he appeared to him at first, "my presence shall go with thee, and I will give thee rest." And Isaiah says, "In all their afflictions he was afflicted, and the Angel of his presence saved them." Ex. xxxiii. 14, and Isa. lxiii. 9. And the Apostle says, referring to the Israelites, "Neither let us tempt Christ as some of them also tempted (him,) and were destroyed of serpents." 1 Cor. x. 9. And again, "Behold, I send an Angel before thee, to keep thee in the way; beware of him, and obey his voice; provoke him not, for he will not pardon your transgressions; for my Name is in him." This is clearly a promise of a distinct divine person, who was to go with them; the same, doubtless, who appeared in the pillar cloud. This whole class of texts is explained still further by referring to Hebrews iii. 1: "Wherefore, holy brethren, partakers of the heavenly calling, consider the Apostle and High Priest of our profession, Christ Jesus." Now the etymology of the term *Apostle* shows that it is identical in signification with angel. But one part of the Apostle's argument in this epistle is to show Christ's superiority to angels; there was, then, a reason why he should not use in this place the ordinary term, but the corresponding one. Both angel and apostle mean one sent. Our Lord repeatedly spoke of himself as one sent, or come from the Father. John iii. 16, 34; vi. 29; x. 36; xx. 21, and elsewhere. The Apostle's argument, and the design of the whole epistle, require that we understand his allusion in this place to be to the Angel of Jehovah—of the divine presence spoken of in the Old Testament. As Christ is emphatically "he whom God hath sent," so he says: Let us consider the Apostle and High Priest of our profession—and we shall see that in christianity we have a Messenger from God, who is higher than the angels of the Old Testament—who is the Angel-

Jehovah himself. The Old Testament saints were believers in the same Redeemer that Stephen saw, standing on the right hand of God. I beg to conclude this subject by quoting the following passages from Dr. Mill and Professor Olshausen:

"The Angel of the Lord who preceded the children of Israel from Egypt, in the cloud and in the fire, was the Lord himself, (agreeably to Ex. xiii. 20, 21, and xiv. 19, 20; Numb. xx. 6, etc.,) possessor of the incommunicable name, Jehovah; and that this Angel of the Covenant, as he is termed in Mal. iii. 1; Gen. xlviii. 15, 16, etc., is the uncreated Word, who appeared in visible form to Jacob and Moses, and who was, in the fulness of time, incarnate in the person of Jesus Christ, is the known undoubted faith of the church of God, and need not to be enlarged on here. This same uncreated Angel, in whom was the name of the Lord, is promised by the mouth of Moses." Olshausen, in one of his tracts on "The deeper sense of scripture," beautifully illustrates the sense in which the old dispensation, the law and the prophets, is fulfilled in the New Testament: "The law, with all its ordinances, is like a grain of seed which includes in itself the whole law of the formation of the plant. Should the plant spring up, the grain of seed must die; a power which would cause it to continue in its isolated subsistence, would be just as destructive as the Judaizing teachers, with whom Paul was forced to contend. But notwithstanding such a fact, the law of the germ which lives no longer, invisibly penetrates the entire plant; so that in the plant's concentrated formations, the law, renewing its youth, repeatedly presents itself again in the fruit. Thus the law was apparently dissolved by Christ, but only in order to be fulfilled in its spirit in every iota."

In conclusion, 1. Our aim in this chapter, as in the third,

has been to vindicate the plan of God's revelation as well as the revelation itself, by showing that infinite wisdom has not made any mistake in the different dispensations from Adam to Christ. Our blessed Lord never let a hint fall from his lips that any part of the Old Testament was done away. On the contrary, he made it the basis of all his teachings, as did his apostles after him. And throughout his whole ministry, he represents himself as fulfilling in his person and office, the scheme of divine love as revealed in the law and the Psalms and the prophets. The Old Testament and his own sayings are alike imperishable. (See Matt. xxiv. 35; and Luke xxiv. 44.) He came into the world to fulfil all righteousness and make an end of transgression by offering himself a sacrifice to God, to satisfy divine justice, and reconcile us to God. And in doing this all things were fulfilled which were written in the law of Moses, and in the prophets, and in the Psalms concerning him. He came therefore not to annihilate, or abrogate, but to confirm and re-institute—"to build again"—"not to perpetuate the former scheme, but to extend and to develope it." The glorious Architect in the New Testament brings out clearly the original design of the Old Testament, which had not before been so clearly seen. The Old Testament is the basis on which the New is erected, and the stability and completeness of both depend on their connection. The Old was the shadow of good things to come, which gave certain assurance of the reality of the good things to come, and some idea of their nature, size, and proportions. The New Testament is the embodiment and the record of those good things. From Genesis to Malachi we have the outline of the picture, and from Matthew to John the divine, we have its filling up and colouring. And the whole is the record of a great and precious salvation. The whole history of the Jewish people, their ritual and government, is one grand prophecy of the future Redeemer. The Old Testament is as full of the Messiah, the age of the world considered, as the New Testament is full of Christ.

"Abraham, the saint, rejoiced of old
When visions of the Lord he saw;
Moses, the man of God, foretold
This great fulfiller of his law.

"The types bore witness to his name,
Obtained their chief design, and ceased:
The incense and the bleeding lamb,
The ark, the altar, and the priest."

2. Let us then study the Old Testament as well as the New. "The word of God, which is contained in the Old and New Testaments, is the only rule to direct us how we may glorify and enjoy him."

Valuable helps for studying the Bible are now happily within the reach of Sabbath-school teachers and the heads of families. Bible dictionaries, concordances, maps of the holy land, Bible illustrations, and oriental travels may be consulted with great advantage. But above all, let us ever pray for the illumination of the divine Spirit on the sacred page, and let us search it with the docility and trustfulness of a little child.

3. One can hardly fail to be impressed, as we are studying the Bible, especially the record of patriarchal times, and of the appearance of the angel of the Lord, with the idea that we are very near to God. We seem to see his form among the trees of Eden, and to hear his voice as he calls to Abraham on Mount Moriah. The riven peaks of Mount Sinai seem yet to speak of his awful glory. It was the Lord's hand that shut Noah into the ark, and as an angel he talked with the patriarchs, and by his Spirit, he dwelt

in the prophets. But in the New Testament we are brought nearer still to God—to God on a throne of mercy, whence we may obtain forgiveness and grace for every time of need.

4. The lives of Old Testament worthies in such close communion with God breathe also a pilgrim-like air. They declared plainly that they were seeking a better country, that is, an heavenly; and God was not ashamed to be called their God, for he hath prepared for them a city. See Hebrews xi. Are we then like them, pilgrims and strangers? Is our home in heaven? Our home is where our heart and treasures are. But as our life is a journey, on what road do we travel, and whither does it lead? On the busy, dusty, jostling high road of humanity, we find many turns and many rough places, and many a weary hour and many a dark and heavy storm lowers over it. But cheer up, fellow pilgrim, many are on the same road with you. Many have travelled it before you, who are now safely arrived in glory. There is one who passed along this same road, travelling in the greatness of his strength, and as he overcame, so does he give grace and glory to all who follow in his footsteps. You are every hour coming nearer to your home, where storms will cease, and the weary will be for ever at rest. If the night is long and dark, the morning will only be the more joyful. If, as pilgrims, you endure hardships in the wilderness, the land of promise will be all the more pleasant because of these trials by the way.

5. How truly astonishing is the divine condescension! The long-suffering of our God is our salvation. As he has been pleased to give us the sacred word, we are not to expect angelic visitors to teach us our duty. The divine word is a sufficient rule to teach us what to believe, and what to do, to be saved. The spirit that was in the prophets and

apostles is promised to us. The great Messiah has come. We have seen his glory, as of the only begotten of the Father. And are we not, some of us, witnesses of his grace and truth—that he hath power on earth to forgive sin? Let us ever adore him as our Saviour, and to him be glory for ever. Amen.

# CHAPTER VI.

## THE FAMILY SACRIFICE AND CONFERENCE.

"—— In his face
Terror and sweetness laboured for the place:
Sometimes his sun-bright eyes would shine so fierce
As if their pointed beams would even pierce
The soul and strike the amaz'd beholder dead;
Sometimes their glory would disperse and spread
More easy flame, and like the star that stood
O'er Bethlehem, promise and portend some good:
Mixt was his bright aspect, as if his breath
Had equal errands both of life and death:
Glory and mildness seemed to contend
In his fair eyes."—*Quarles.*

In Judges xiii. 10, 11, the angel is called a man. In this the writer follows the woman, and both speak of him, as he appeared to them. As soon as the angel appeared the second time to the woman, she respectfully entreated that he would wait till she could go and fetch her husband; and having obtained assurance that he would tarry, she runs for Manoah. The pious of those days were familiar with angelic visitors, who appeared in the form and usual dress of prophets or men of God. Sometimes they were distinguished by a peculiar majesty and sublimity of appearance. Pictures of angels still represent them with a glory around their head. It is only in the emblematic descriptions of them, that they are said to have wings. It is a mistake to represent this angel with wings and in a white robe, as is generally done.

In verses twelve and fourteen, Manoah responds amen to all the angel says. As if he had said, Let all you have promised to my wife come to pass. I believe. "But how shall we order the child, and how shall we do unto him?" or as it is in the Hebrew, What shall be the *rule* by which we shall govern and teach him? In the fifteenth and twenty-first verses, inclusive, we have the conference of the angel with Manoah and his wife, and their sacrifice, and the angel's ascent into heaven.

Bread, in the sixteenth verse, is to be taken, as it is often in the Bible, for food in general. (2 Kings vi. 22, 23; Matt. vi. 11.) It is not easy to see the connection of this verse, if we suppose that all the conversation is recorded. If all is written that passed between them, then this verse seems to be an answer to what was in Manoah's mind, rather than a reply to anything he had actually said. The same thing is found in the New Testament. Our Lord several times replies to what was in the minds of his hearers, rather than to any objection stated, or question really put, so far as the record goes.

The angel does not deny that he was a man, nor does he deny that he was God. He speaks to Manoah in the character that he knew Manoah understood him to be, and reminds him that sacrifices must be offered to Jehovah only. Just as when our Lord said in reply to one who addressed him as "good Master," "Why callest thou me good? there is none good but one, that is God." He did not deny that he was God, or affirm that he was not himself good, the supreme goodness. He meant to say, So supreme in goodness is God, that comparatively it is not proper to say that any one else is good; and besides, if I am really what you say I am, then why do you not receive my testimony? In all such places, the answer is obviously made according to the state of the mind of the person addressed, and not intended to express the truth as known to the speaker. The angel replies therefore to Manoah according to the light Manoah had. He does not forbid him to sacrifice, nor does he tell him he must not sacrifice to him. He does remind him, however, that if he offered sacrifice, it must be to God. As though he had said to him, Be careful that your sacrifice be in sincerity and truth, and in just the way that God has appointed; otherwise it will not be acceptable in his sight. The angel says, I have no need of this food And if you are going to offer a sacrifice, offer it to Jehovah only. There is then no angel worship here. Manoah may have intended a mere act of hospitality first, and that then they would unite together in worship, and offer up a part of it as a burnt-offering. Manoah may have remembered how Abraham offered to render worship before an angel, and have desired to imitate him. And yet he was in doubt, if indeed he had any suspicion of the angelic character of his visitor. He did not yet know that he was an angel of the Lord. And besides, if he had intended to worship an angel, he did not do so. The apostle John, and the prophet Daniel also, we remember, were prevented from rendering homage to angels.

The objection that Manoah was not a priest, and therefore had no right to offer sacrifice, belongs to that obsolete idea, that almighty grace is straitened, and can flow only in one narrow channel. He who made Melchizedek a priest and king, could make Manoah a priest. The command or permission of the angel was sufficient authority, and the acceptance of the offering is proof that it was rightly done. Christ Jesus himself is a priest not after the Aaronic model. He came not of the tribe of Levi. And yet he is exalted above all lawgivers, priests, and angels, and set down at the right hand of God, a Prince and a Saviour and a Priest to appear in the presence of God for us.

"What is thy name?" In the Bible *name* is sometimes equivalent to *nature*, *essence*, and *glory*. Is Manoah rebuked here for unhallowed curiosity? I do not see wherein he was guilty. There is nothing intended to be improper, impertinent, or irreverent in his manner or language. Nor does it appear that he had been told before, or could have learned in any way, that the name of the visitor was not to be known, but was "secret," wonderful, ineffable. The same Hebrew word here translated *secret* is rendered *wonderful*, as has been already stated, in Isaiah ix. 6; where it is most unquestionably applied to the Messiah, who is Christ. The idea expressed here is one of wonder at superhuman works, or on beholding miraculous interpositions. And Manoah and his wife looked on in astonishment, as "the angel did wondrously." Bush's paraphrase is to the point: "You have scarcely any real occasion to inquire as to my name, (nature;) it is obvious from the words, promises, and actions already witnessed and yet further to be displayed, that I am, and am therefore to be called, Peli, the admirable one, the great worker of wonders, the master of miracles. The original has the form of a proper name, but the force of an appellative." May not the angel have wished to convey to their mind that he was the angel promised in Ex. xxiii. 20, 21? Have we here anything more than an epitome of the conversation held between the angel and Manoah and his wife? For the true character of this angel, see the preceding chapter.

The meat-offering, in the nineteenth verse, is not a happy translation. It should be a "flour-offering," such as the law prescribed. "And offered it upon a rock," just as Gideon did. Detached rocks of the proper size for a table or an altar abound throughout the country. Mounds of earth or stones were used as altars in the earliest times. And while Manoah and his wife were offering their sacrifice unto the Lord, "the angel did wondrously." Angel is not in the original, but it is rightly supplied. There is no doubt of the meaning. It was the angel that did wondrously. The angel acted according to his name. Being wonderful in his nature, it was natural for him to perform wonderful things. What the wonders were, we are not told. Probably among the things which he did was to manifest more of his divine glory, and to cause fire to fall from heaven, as on Abraham's sacrifice, and Elijah's; or to come out of the rock to consume the offering, as the angel did who appeared to Gideon. As the smoke of the sacrifice went up toward heaven, the angel ascended in the flames, as if they were his chariot. And now Manoah's conviction is perfect. His mind no doubt had been gradually opening to the truth. But now he knew that he was an angel of the Lord.

"And Manoah said unto his wife, We shall surely die, because we have seen God."

1. Here is a domestic conference, in which the wife is the best counsellor. A common notion prevailed among the ancient Jews that it was death to see the face of God, or of an unveiled angel. Manoah's fears were probably excited by this prevailing notion. He may indeed have had in his mind what the Lord said to Moses, when he entreated to see his glory: "Thou canst not see my face; for there shall no man see me and live." Jacob also speaks of his wrestling with the angel, and of his having seen God face to face, and yet his life was preserved, as something wonderful. Gen. xxxii. 29, 30. Manoah's apprehensions then were not wholly groundless, yet we cannot but admire the faith and composure of his wife.

2. Manoah's alarm was true to fallen humanity. Guilt

is always suspicious. Adam and Eve were afraid and hid themselves when they heard the voice of the Lord God in the garden. So Manoah and his wife, instead of looking up to heaven thankfully, fell down upon the earth half dead with fear. It is our infirmity to pervert divine blessings into omens of evil. Our eyes are so weak that we are confounded with what should comfort us. We are prone to find death in the vision that God gives us announcing life. We write bitter things, while God writes unspeakably precious promises. The limits of grace and goodness are made by ourselves, and not by our heavenly Father. He is infinitely better to us than our own fears. His mercies surpass our largest hopes. The gospel offer is made to us in perfect good faith. Salvation is always of the Lord, and damnation is always the sinner's own work. The guilt of perdition rests on the sinner's own head. God is a sovereign. Grace is sufficient, and the sinner is free.

3. The wife's reply is nobly put and ably applied. Her reasoning is remarkably correct. Her theology is as sound as if she had been educated by the Synod of Dort, or by the Westminster Assembly of Divines. It is precisely the style of reasoning David adopted when he was in trouble. He often calls upon his soul to hope in God for the future, by remembering the divine goodness in times past. Moses used the same plea for an extension of divine forbearance and patience towards the rebellious Israelites. And Paul used the same train of argument to prove the final and complete triumph of a believer. "God commendeth his love toward us, in that while we were yet sinners, Christ died for us. Much more then, being now justified by his blood, we shall be saved from wrath through him. For if when we were sinners, we were reconciled to God by the death of his Son; much more, being reconciled, we shall be saved by his life." Rom. v. 8–10

"But his wife said unto him, If the Lord were pleased to kill us, he would not have received a burnt-offering and a meat-offering at our hands." This the husband in his panic seems to have forgotten. But the wife continues to remind him how the Lord had showed them also all things concerning the birth and education of their son, and had told them of the great commission he was to execute as Israel's deliverer. Hence she concluded it could not be that they were to die. The accomplishment of the promise implies that the Lord would not kill them. If the Lord were pleased to kill us now, he would not have shown us such things as these at this time.

It is a safe method for us to follow—to plead God's past mercies as a ground of hope for the future. His rule is grace upon grace. He that has, receives more. It is not irreverent to say that he who gave his Son for us, will with him give us all things. Is it then reasonable to fear that he who has preserved us forty years will fail us for the next twenty, if our pilgrimage should continue so long? He who made you, aged friend, and gave his Son to redeem you, will not suffer you to perish for the want of meaner things. And the feeling of your need of his grace, is a proof that he is waiting to be gracious. Even the anxious inquiry after salvation proves that the work is already begun. Penitential pangs are not natural, but gracious, and argue that God has laid his hand upon us. And he is a rock. All his works are perfect. He will not leave his work of grace half finished. Nor would he have told us such things of his love and grace—he would not have manifested such unwillingness to destroy the impenitent, as we find in the Scriptures, nor have exercised such long-suffering and patience as we see in history and in the events of every day life, if he did not offer pardon and eternal life to us in perfect good faith on the terms propounded in the gospel.

And surely the argument from past experience should be a satisfactory one. Experience worketh hope, and hope maketh not ashamed. Romans v. 4, 5. Is it not an impeachment of the divine sincerity, to fear that if God begins a good work, he will not complete it? If he has preserved us so long—borne with our waywardness and pardoned our transgressions, may we not trust him, for time to come? May we not trust in the loving-kindness of him who so loved us as to give his Son to redeem us? It cannot be that supreme benevolence tantalizes us—keeps us as the Philistines did Samson to make sport of us on some great occasion. If so, why has he ever opened our hearts to our need of salvation? Why do we feel our guilt, and desire to escape from the wrath to come? Surely he would not have showed us all these things, nor would he at this time have told us such things as these, if the Lord were pleased to kill us. Surely he would not have announced to us the glad tidings of the gospel—would not have made to us such full and free offers of mercy, if he were not pleased to accept us. Surely there is honesty in the declaration: "It is a faithful saying, and worthy of all acceptation, that Jesus Christ came into the world to save sinners"—even the chief of sinners. God's acceptance of the sacrifice of his Son, Jesus Christ, is a positive proof that his merits and mediation are available for us. According to the Scriptures, Christ died for our sins and rose again for our justification, and now appears in the presence of God for us as our High Priest and ever-living Intercessor. Paul, in all his epistles, but especially in the epistle to the Hebrews, insists upon the fact that Christ is now seated at the right hand of the throne of God, as conclusive that he is superior to Moses and Aaron and all the angels. And the evidence moreover of his acceptance at the right hand of God is rendered complete by the coming of the Holy Spirit to take of the things which are his, and show them unto us—convincing the world of sin, of righteousness, and of judgment. And since God has not withheld from us his only Son, but hath commended his love to us, in that he gave his Son to die for us, while we were yet his enemies; how much more will he not give us all things on account of the gift of his Son? Wherefore we beseech you in Christ's stead, be ye reconciled to God; for he hath made him to be sin—a sin-offering—for us, though he knew no sin, that we might be made the righteousness of God in him. Wherefore Jesus also, that he might sanctify the people with his own blood, suffered without the gate. Let us go forth therefore unto him without the camp, bearing his reproach. Heb. xiii. 12, 13.

# CHAPTER VII.

## THE LIFE OF THE HERO BEGUN.

"There are tones that will haunt us, though lonely
Our path be o'er mountain or sea;
There are looks that will part from us only
When memory ceases to be;
There are hopes which our burden can lighten,
Though toilsome and steep be the way;
And dreams that, like moonlight, can brighten
With a light that is clearer than day."

"AND the woman bare a son, and called his name Samson." The original is *Shimshon*, from the root *shamash*, to serve. The Hebrew for sun, *Shemesh*, is probably from the same root, and means a little servant, that is, a little sun. But why did they call him Shimshon (Samson)? What relation had he to the sun? Schmid and others say his parents so called him in allusion to the shining of the angel's face, like the sun, when he first appeared to his mother. Others, and more properly, say, because of the resplendent brightness that surrounded the angel as he ascended out of their sight, after the sacrifice. Some assume that maternal fondness selected this name as a proper one for an only son. As there is but one sun, so she would have but one Samson. By whatever process his parents arrived at the name, whether by the etymology or derivation hinted at, or by some other, they no doubt intended the name of their child to be expressive of their gratitude, and a proof of their pious acknowledgment of the divine favour shown them.

Samson's history, like that of Esau and Ishmael, begins before his birth, and like that of Moses, Samuel, and Solomon, is recorded from his birth. Like Jeremiah, he was set apart to a great work from his mother's womb. There seems, however, to have been nothing extraordinary in the manner of his birth. The child is always father to the man; but in some this is more apparent than in others. It was so with Samson. "The presages of the womb and the cradle are commonly answered in the life; it is not the use of God to cast away strange beginnings."—*Hall.*

The record of his childhood and early youth, which is also true of many of the world's great men, is scant. He grew, "and the Lord blessed him." That is, such divine blessings rested on him that it was plainly to be seen he was under God's peculiar protection. We cannot help feeling, however, some desire to know more of his boyhood, that we might see how the child was father to the man. The man was most extraordinary; how was the boy? Did his companions, in the streets of Zorah, nameless and unknown, see anything in the long-haired boy that predicted he was to be the lion-killer, and the slayer of the lords of the Philistines?

"And the Lord blessed him"—caused him to grow in stature and strength. External providences favoured him, and he was under internal divine influences.

"And the Spirit of the Lord began to move him at times in the camp of Dan, between Zorah and Eshtaol." That is, while he was yet young—yet at home with his parents, and subject unto them, the Spirit of God moved on his heart, causing him to feel the humiliation of his countrymen, the hatefulness of their subjection to such a people as the Philistines, and exciting in him strong desires to do something for their deliverance. From his tenderest years God began to prepare him for the work to which he was called. It was a great honour to have something to do, and a great mercy to be prepared to do it. The divine influence on him, I apprehend, was both gracious and miraculous. True, the power to work miracles, and the gift of prophecy, were not always and necessarily connected with an experience of grace. They ought, indeed, always to have been found united; but historically we know they were not. Nor are eminent gifts and attainments now always found in connection with personal piety. When the Spirit of the Lord moved the child Samson, I suppose we are to understand that he was regenerated, and that such ideas were put into his youthful mind, and such strength imparted to his growing frame, as God saw would best fit him for his future work. And it is just so still. It is as true now as it ever was, that God renews the heart by his Spirit, and by his providence prepares us for the work to which he calls us in this world. The Holy Spirit that moved the patriarchs, and prophets, and judges, in days of old, is not another Holy Spirit, but the same, the very same, that came down on the day of Pentecost, and that opened the heart of Lydia at Philippi, and dwelt in Paul and in John the divine. Regeneration is always an act of omnipotence. True holiness is never produced in us but by the Spirit of God. The only difference between the moving of the Spirit of God upon the heart of a child now and among us, and upon Samson, lies in the bearing that it had in his case upon his mission as a judge and an avenger of his people. The Holy Spirit was bestowed in an extraordinary measure in Old Testament times, upon those persons whom the Lord had chosen to perform great deeds for the deliverance of his people.

The original for "began to move him at times," is peculiar. According to Diodati, it means, to inspire magnanimous thoughts into him, and give him a miraculous strength of body and courage, and to incite him to do great and more than human acts. The radical word means an anvil, and the metaphor seems to be drawn from the repeated and somewhat violent shocks of the smith's hammer. Thus did the Spirit of the Lord stir up Samson. His call was clear, repeated, and urgent.

The twenty-fifth verse seems to say that a camp was formed between Zorah and Eshtaol, to give some check to the Philistines; and when the Hebrews went out for drill, or to make a demonstration against the enemy, young Samson went out with them, and by various manifestations of strength and courage, gave intimations of what he would do when he should become of age. This was the bright sunny morning of our hero judge. Alas! that it was so short. He grew, and the Spirit of the Lord began to move him, inspiring him with the purpose and preparing him for the deliverance of his people. The sequel discloses, however, the painful fact that Samson did not meet the possibilities of his destiny. His character was not equal to his gifts. His history is a riddle, the unravelling of which is a warning of great significance to young men, especially to such as have had pious parents, and begun life with high religious hopes. His name is a miracle and a by-word—a glory and a shame—proclaiming divine sovereignty and mercy, and at the same time the awful severity of divine goodness.

As Samson's manhood is not such as his youth promised, let no child of pious parents push away this history, and say, I shall never disappoint my parents. Do we not read of one who, with quite as much indignation as it is prudent for any young man to express, said, in reference to a wicked thing, "Is thy servant a dog that he should do this thing?" and yet he did that very thing. Your baptismal covenant, young man, can hardly bind you more strictly than Samson's circumcision and Nazaritish vows bound him. Nor have you any right to conclude that the gracious movements of

God's Spirit will be more effectual and persistent in you than they were in him. It is true, you may have had advantages which he had not—and yet it is equally true that many young people, brought up as piously as yourselves, have forgotten their Bibles, and forsaken the house of God, and made shipwreck of the faith and hope of their parents.

It is painfully true that some of the children of great promise, and high hopes, have turned out very badly. Their sun has gone down into the night of sorrow and death, while yet it was high noon; nor have they fallen alone. They have crushed the hearts of their parents, and brought their gray hairs with sorrow to the grave. Let the biography of this extraordinary man, then, be a warning to all the young, of the terrific whirlpools, and sunken rocks, on which so many adventurers have made shipwreck for time and eternity.

The principles taught in the foregoing remarks, and suggested by the early training of our hero, are of universal importance; but especially so in a new country, and in the infancy of a State. A great teaching philosopher of antiquity* asserts, and correctly, too, that he who is about to be a good man in anything whatever, ought immediately, from childhood, to practise, when engaged in playful and serious pursuits, the very things suited to the particular object he has in view. Plato's idea is, that he who is about to make himself a good farmer, should have playthings that teach him about the tilling of the ground. And he that is to be a house-builder, should play at building children's houses. And his parents or guardian should provide him with the implements, as toys, that should teach him familiarity with the future employment of the tools belonging tc the art he is to pursue. The teacher of children should en

* Plato, the Laws, book I.

deavour to make the plays and pleasures of the child introductory to his future life. If a boy is to be a soldier, he should be taught to walk, ride, endure fatigue, and the like things in his sports. The child should be taught what he is to do when he is a man. This principle is generally acknowledged, and yet among nominal christians nothing is more apparent than the neglect of children at home. It is not merely the neglect of family religion that I deplore, but of all proper family nurture and admonition. I am thoroughly persuaded that a very large proportion of the lawlessness, iniquity, and corruption of the times may be traced to the want of subordination and instruction in our families. The hope of the state and of the church is of necessity centered in the young. It is a most imperative duty, then, to bring them up in the way they should go. In wisdom the Creator has arranged that the family should be the first and greatest of all educational agencies. The home, and then the school room, and the house of worship, are instrumentalities that make us what we are. The home is first and most important; there is the root that feeds the life; there the precious metal is first moulded into shape which may afterwards be rasped and polished, but not recast. There lines may be traced on a yielding and pliable nature, that become as enduring as if sculptured on stone. The lessons of our earliest home are wrought into the structure of the mind, and give to it shape and colouring more or less indestructible. The mind of the little one, in the mother's arms, is like a daguerreotype plate, that receives whatever image is first cast upon it. No subsequent impressions can ever be so distinct. And so susceptible is the tender mind, that it is ever taking impressions. In the granite rocks we find preserved from ages so long past that we cannot name their date, impressions of the tiniest leaves of the forest. So it is often the case that words uttered carelessly sink into the soul, and may be traced upon its every fibre for ever afterwards, as if written with a pen of iron, and the point of a diamond. A breath covers the frosted window with an icy film, and a word, or a cruel suspicion, or a wicked gesture or picture, may for ever crust the mirror of a young heart. But not only is the young heart peculiarly susceptible of impressions, but it is, alas! prone to evil rather than good. This is true of all men until they are taught of God. But in the young there is a peculiar aptitude to receive good impressions. Evil habits are not then formed; the passions are not then glowing like a furnace; evil associations have not then pre-occupied the affections. This is the time to open the heart to truth, and turn it to God. These opportunities are beyond all price. Hear the lesson, parents and Sabbath-school teachers.

All history, all analogy, and all experience prove that institutions alone cannot keep a people free. It is in the intelligence, social morality, and religious spirit of the people that lies the hope of our continuing to have a free and salutary form of government. It is as plain and true as that there is a sun in the heavens, pouring his light upon our fields and mountains, and ripening our fruits and harvests, that our rapid growth and great prosperity are to be ascribed to moral causes—our religiousness of character, and our free and wisely constructed institutions. Whenever we lose our social ethics and religious spirit, we shall find the days of the Republic numbered, and the reign of corruption, anarchy, and tyranny commenced.

Family training is a theme that cannot be exhausted. Even when nothing new is elicited in urging its importance, it is well to bring old truths again and again before the public. As in building the pyramids, stone was laid upon stone, and course upon course, until the huge pile arose, and then it was finished from the top downwards; so at home and in earliest years the work of education is begun. And long afterwards, by line upon line, and precept upon precept, here a little and there a little, the mind is developed, and the moral character formed. The importance of proper training at home, and in earliest years, is greatly enhanced among us by the fact that our country is in a great measure governed by young men, and that our young men leave home early; and yet almost all the education many of them receive is obtained at home and from the primary school. And when they leave home they are exposed to many dangers: they are not only from home, but many of them are without proper female society; they are in the season of the passions; they are ambitious of fame and wealth. It is vastly important, therefore, that they be well established in right moral principles. How else can we expect them to resist the fascinations of vice, or escape the corruption of a weakened moral sense, from the infidelity that prevails around them? Much has been done by our schools, lyceums, lecturings, libraries, and pulpit efforts, for the young, but we are not satisfied. The results attained are not commensurate with our hopes, nor with the urgencies of the case. Crime is still on the increase. The present course of a very large number of our youth—I dare not say how large a proportion—is not hopeful. The future of American youth, physically, mentally, and socially, is not hopeful. The prospect is one of diminished stature and strength. The hastening to be rich, the excess, and extravagance, and dissipation of the present generation are likely to entail feebleness and luxury on that which is to come; nor is this true only of those who have had vicious parents. The ranks of such are every day increasing from the thresholds of piety. Are there not now among the profane many that were brought up in the homes of industry and prayer? We do not read aright if violence and forgery, intemperance and lewdness, profane and obscene language, robberies, murders, divorces, and suicides, have not become so common as hardly to awaken our surprise. The society of our day is diseased—it is corrupt—it is rotten—it is "a shame and a lie." A fearful malady is at work, and sad consequences are to be apprehended. Thinking men, earnest minded, large hearted men are sad, and some are even despairing. How is it that so much parental love and care, anxiety and toil, produce no more fruits? In the next generation, who are to be our successful merchants, our legislators, statesmen, and learned and great men? If the morning of life is neglected, if the young are physically debilitated, and morally depraved, and their minds dark and ignorant, how can we avoid a rapid movement on the downward road?

To have any fears on such a subject is painful to a well disposed mind. It fills us with horror to think of the calamities that are, sooner or later, measured out to corrupt communities by a retributive Providence. As parents and patriots, and much more as christians, we should consider the dangerous tendencies of excessive devotion to money-making and sensual delights. If parents are devoted to an increase of stocks and dividends, so as to neglect the mind and social affections—if their ambition is to occupy a palatial residence, keep a superb equipage, and deck their daughters in the stiffest crinolines, richest furs, and most costly silks, and have their sons drive the fastest horses, and drink the most costly wines—then what will their grandchildren be, if they have any? Will not the spirit of the fathers become stronger, and more sordid, and more injurious as it descends to the children? What, then, can be done?

1. A more healthy, vigorous kind of literature can be put into the hands of the young. In popularizing science,

our school systems are almost emasculated. Our children are fed on pap, when they should have honest hard bread and sound meat. In making a royal road to scholarship easy, we have denied them the gymnastics of the mind, and too many of them have stumbled over the ass's bridge, or are standing still upon it. The Peter Parley literature of our schools should be exiled to the islands of the southern Pacific.

2. Our children should be taught, everywhere and always, that knowledge, mental power, discipline of thought, and not a mere parrot recital at an examination, is the thing to be gained by going to school. Dr. Johnson said that it was a great thing gained when a child knew there was such a place as Kamschatka. All knowledge tends to profit.

3. Family government and training must be resumed. One of the sources of the evils of the times is in the relaxed state of family government. As the common schools and Sabbath-schools have prevailed, and have been made to take the place of family teachings, so the influence of parents has diminished. Now if the common schools and Sabbath-schools are made substitutes for family government, then it were a misfortune that they have ever been established. It is not their vocation to take the child altogether from parental training. Their true place is auxiliary to the parent. They are to help the parent, but not to supersede him, or in the smallest degree weaken his influence.

4. In the family training of children there must be a more earnest, simple inculcation of moral precepts. In becoming enlightened and liberal, we must distinguish between a proper regard for religious truth and absolute indifference. The religious principles of the families of a nation give character to its morals and mental activities. All the blessings of civilized life may be traced to our private dwellings—to our homes and to our mothers. The corner stones of

our churches and of the state are our hearthstones, guarded by lawfully wedded forms of conjugal love. "Let our temples," says one, "crumble, and our academies decay; let every public edifice, our halls of justice, and our capitals of state, be levelled with the dust, but spare our homes. Let no socialist invade them with his wild plans of community. Man did not invent, and he cannot improve or abrogate them. A private shelter to cover in two hearts dearer to each other than all in the world; high walls, to exclude the profane eyes of human beings; seclusion enough for children to feel that mother is a holy and a peculiar name—this is home; and here is the birth place of every virtuous impulse, and every sacred thought. Here the church and the state must come for their origin and their support. Oh, spare our homes!"

Yes, our *homes* must be cherished as the most sacred spots we have on earth. Here we may teach our children how to regain ten thousand little Edens, by inspiring them with a love for the beauties of nature and of art, and with love to mankind and their blessed Creator. I should have been an atheist, said John Randolph, but for the recollection that my mother used to take my little hands in hers, and cause me to say, on her knees, "Our Father which art in heaven." But to make home the fountain of such influences, it must be truly the seat of the affections. Some parents seem to move among their tender olive plants with so much haughty dignity, and cold precision, that they remind me of the lofty and craggy peaks of the icebergs that are sometimes found floating among the island gardens of the tropics. Their presence is always known by the chilliness of the air. I am persuaded it were better to put out our children's eyes than to crush their affections in the nursery. It were better that a whole family were carried off by the plague, than that it should live without a heart.

Rather let the young heart burst out in glee, and song, and sympathy. Teach the little one to hate only " sin, dirt, and the devil," and to love everything beautiful and good. Let the warm emotions of the little heir to immortality gush out for the cow that gives him milk, and for the dog that guards his father's door, and allows his tiny fingers to pinch his ears. Teach your children to hate vice, and to love the robin and the rose, their country and their God, and then you may commit the government to their shoulders. And let the young prize the principles of their pious parents, and heed their solemn warnings against the fascinations of vice.

"—Prize them, brother, 'twill not last for ever,
And once escaped, it will return—no ! never !
It is the morning : work while lasts its light;
Ye cannot toil so cheerily at night.
It is the time of sowing; let the seed
Produce the harvest that your soul will need.
And 'tis the planting time; be sure the root
Be such as bears the most delicious fruit."

# CHAPTER VIII.

## SAMSON'S FIRST LOVE AND THE LION-FIGHT.

"Yet truth to say, I oft have heard men wonder
Why thou shouldst wed Philistian women rather
Than of thine own tribe, fairer, or as fair,
At least of thy own nation, and as noble."

*Samson Agonistes.*

IN the last chapter we had a glance at the early piety of the great Israelite. The spirit of God was upon him in the camp of his countrymen, near his native city. His religion, however, does not seem to have flourished long. His journeys to Timnath, though marked with deeds of miraculous strength, are the beginnings of his trouble.

The fourteenth chapter tells us how he went down to Timnath, and fell in love with a Philistine damsel. Timnath was near the sea side, hence the expression went down. Though this city belonged to his own tribe, it was at this time in the hands of the Philistines. It had once belonged to Judah, but had been transferred to Dan. It was some fifteen miles north-east of Eshtaol, and twenty west from Jerusalem. Its possession now by the Philistines was a reproach to the Israelites. Either they had not driven them out originally, as they should have done in the time of the conquest under Joshua and Caleb, or the Philistines had returned and re-occupied it. However this may have been, there was at this time free intercourse between the Philistines and the Hebrews. The population was probably mixed, but the Hebrews were under tribute to the Philistines.

In considering Samson's choice of a wife, we are conscious of a feeling of painful disappointment. We had a right to expect Manoah's son would have made a better selection. In choosing a Philistine, we begin to see his lower nature acting the tyrant. But it were well if domestic history in modern times did not present many instances of similar stubborness. In such matters, the fancy of young people is often the supreme law. Louis XIV. was not more headstrong and dogmatic when he said, that his heavy guns were the last reason of kings, than is the mere fancy of the eye in youth. Samson's falling in love, was in the ordinary way: "And he saw a woman of Timnath," and she pleased him well. Hebrew, She was just right in his eyes. Some interpreters think the original implies something more than she was agreeable to his fancy. Possibly it may mean, that he was moved by the Lord to this alliance, seeing that it would furnish a proper occasion for him to begin his deliverances. The Hebrew *yashar* may mean not only that she was beautiful, fascinating in his eyes, but also that she was fit, right, appropriate in regard to the great work which he had to accomplish. If this sense be adopted here, then Samson was prophet enough to understand the popular doctrine of availability. He had regard to an ulterior and higher purpose than gratifying his taste. This does not necessarily imply, however, that he did not love this woman. Prudence and affection may co-exist. Nor do I see anything wrong in his making his love for this woman subservient to the great patriotic mission for which Providence had raised him up. But surely it was a strange beginning. The promised deliverer of Israel takes a wife from their hereditary enemies. But was not this a fair prologue to the rest of his life? He was a man of paradoxes.

We do not wonder that his pious parents were astonished at his wish to take a Philistine woman to wife. They were national enemies. And the angel had said he should deliver Israel. They would therefore naturally inquire, How is this? Is our deliverance to begin with an alliance? We are not to touch anything unclean; our child is a Nazarite; and yet he wishes to marry a heathen! This is the beginning of the riddle. "Is there never a woman among thy brethren?" is the natural inquiry of such a father and mother. As he was so especially consecrated to God, it must have seemed peculiarly improper for him to make such an alliance. But Samson was not in a reasoning mood. His love for the Philistine maid was as ardent as his strength was great. The brave love heroically. As a good son, he consults his parents, and asks their approbation; but, then as is too often the case, he pressed his own desires too obstinately. When his parents remonstrated against such an alliance, he replied to his father, saying, "Get her for me, for she pleaseth me well." Still, let us not forget that he did consult his parents. This showed his regard for them and for the law of God. Before he paid his addresses to the young woman, or said anything to her parents, he laid the affair before his own parents. As yet his marrying was not a foregone conclusion. Thus far he is a noble example for all young persons. Doubtless there would be many more happy marriages, if pious parents were more reverentially consulted, and if such unions were more generally formed with due regard to the divine will. Obedience to God in marrying, as well as in other things, is the way of happiness.

In seeking a Philistine wife, even in the most favourable view we can take of the affair, Samson was treading on doubtful and dangerous ground. Their law expressly forbade the Israelites to marry among those nations that were cursed and devoted to destruction. It does not appear, however, that the Philistines were numbered among the doomed Canaanites. They were of Egyptian origin. The spirit of the Hebrew law, however, was plainly against such alliances, for the Philistines were idolators and foreigners. It is true the law that forbade an Israelite to marry a heathen, was a ceremonial law, or a police law—one that related to their national policy. It was not one of the laws of the decalogue. It was not a moral law. It might therefore be changed, or suspended.

In what sense was it "of the Lord" that he sought the Timnite damsel for a wife as an occasion against the Philistines? It is seldom the sacred writers give reasons for what they record, but the fourth verse seems to be parenthetical, and designed to explain why Samson's parents declined consenting to this marriage. It is clearly implied that if they had known that this was God's will, they would at once have acquiesced. They did agree to go with him to Timnath, as we find from the following verse, to see more about the matter, and finally gave their consent. Some think they went with Samson because he told them plainly his motives, or that in some way, they understood the thing was of the Lord. But if the divine prohibition against such an alliance was repealed for the time, making for special reasons his case an exception, how is it that the historian does not inform us of this fact? Why does not Samson tell his parents that the law is repealed in this case? There is not even a hint of any such thing. The statement that this alliance was of the Lord does not excuse Samson from all responsibility. The match was of his own seeking. He acted as a free agent in going down to Timnath. He was not carried there by angels, nor did God miraculously excite his love towards the Philistine dame. But God, seeing Samson's choice, determined to bring good out of it—he determined that his attachment to a Philistine woman should be overruled, so as to be the occasion of his beginning to deliver Israel.

That it was of the Lord, that he sought an occasion against the Philistines, does not make God the author of it. Samson was permitted to exercise his own free will, and to follow his fancy in choosing a wife, and God, in the exercise of free agency and sovereignty, made his choice subservient to the fulfilment of the promise made to his mother, that he should begin to deliver Israel from the hands of the Philistines. The Philistines were a people already tried and under sentence of judgment in the court of heaven. *Against* is here used in the sense of *from, concerning* them. The fault of a conflict was to come from them, and then they were to be punished for the wrongs they had done to Israel. He, Samson, and not the Lord, is the proper subject of the verb. And even if we are not able to explain why the Lord adopted this peculiar way of bringing down his judgments on the Philistines, the sacred narrative is none the less perfect. It is a simple record of events, or of God's dealings with his people, and not an explanation of motives or a detail of reasons for the divine proceedings. Some suggest that this method was adopted to concentrate on the person of Samson himself the whole wrath and force of the Philistines, because it was God's plan to make him the deliverer of the Hebrews by his own personal exploits, rather than by leading their hosts, as the other judges had done. He was not the chief of their armies, but himself the army, more fully than ever the grand monarch was the state. It was a part of this plan therefore to bring about a private quarrel between Samson and their enemies, and this was done naturally enough, and as many other quarrels have been, about a woman. Helen is not alone in her glory. Other cities than Troy have been exceedingly troubled on account of their fair ones. Whether Samson prophetically foresaw what was to happen is not stated. Most probably he did not know beforehand in what way the result was to be effected. But having full confidence in the providence of God, and knowing that it was his will to execute judgments upon the enemies of his countrymen, and that he was raised up to be the agent of inflicting them, he was no doubt under a strong impression that such results would come of his enterprise, but without any definite idea of the details. God knows the end from the beginning. The divine mind saw, therefore, clearly how the baseness and perfidy of Samson's wife and professed friends would prove an occasion of bitter hatred and revenge—and how the Philistines would thereby lay themselves liable to punishment—and that there was no injustice in their punishment. But the omniscience of the supreme Being was not a moving cause to the actors. They acted of their own free will as in the case of our Lord's crucifixion. And is there any reason why the Almighty may not use his omniscience in governing the world, and in making the wicked work out their own punishment? Some restrict the moving or exciting from the Lord to his seeking a righteous cause of quarrel, and deny that Samson's marriage with the Timnite was in any sense instigated by the Lord. It was of the Lord that Samson should begin his work of delivering the Israelites from the tyranny of their oppressors, and that he should have a just ground for inflicting judgments upon them; but it was not of the Lord that he should violate the law in marrying a heathen. In this view of his case, we find him moved by the Lord to find a quarrel with the Philistines, and constitutionally framed to be a great warrior and an avenger of Hebrew wrongs, and at the same time, we see him moved by his own constitutional and most characteristic propensity to find the cause or occasion of a quarrel with the Philistines by falling in love with one of their maidens and seeking her in marriage. But great care is necessary to distinguish between what the Lord moved him to do, and what his own propensity moved him to do. Think you, that he prayed to God to direct him as to the precise method of his procedure against the Philistines, or being persuaded that it was the divine will for him to seek a quarrel with them, did he trust to his own judgment as to the means; and in the meantime concludes that he will find the occasion of the quarrel in gratifying his passion for a Philistine maid? It is certainly true that men sometimes so deceive themselves, that they pray for guidance from the Lord, while at the same time, their course is fixed in their own hearts. What they will do is a foregone conclusion. They pray for the divine will to be done, and do their own will. They pray for light to follow Providence, and rise from their knees and go straightway out to lead Providence. They bow their knees before God, but not their souls. And regarding iniquity in their hearts, their prayers are not heard. Whatever it does or does not mean, the fourth verse cannot teach that God prompted Samson to transgress. God cannot tempt any man to evil.

"For at that time the Philistines had dominion over Israel." What is the force here of the illative *for?* In some sense it certainly expresses the idea that Samson was moved to find a pretext for avenging his people on their enemies. Schmid, and some others, understand it thus: the Philistines, by the art of war, were the conquerors; they had dominion over the Israelites, and it was not right for them to rebel against existing power, unless some fresh overt act of oppression was committed. The idea, then, is, that though suffering under a tyranny, yet it was necessary for them to have a just cause for endeavouring to shake off the yoke; and that it would have been unlawful for them to rise against their conquerors without such a cause. Our fathers of the Revolution of 1776, sought diligently to justify their Declaration of Independence and separation from the mother country, by stating to the whole world their reasons. They recited the acts of the British Parliament that were unlawful, unjust, and oppressive. They had sought repeatedly, and in various ways, for redress, but in vain. They were spurned from the throne, and their only hope was in revolution. The same is true of the revolution of 1688. It is unquestionably true that the Bible is very strong against insubordination and rebellion. But I have yet to see the proof that it enjoins, absolutely and unconditionally, the duty of passive obedience. The danger of our times, however, is all in the contrary direction. In Samson's case there is at least the appearance of singular prudence and moderation; "that although he had ample grounds in the divine commission implied in the very fact of his being raised up and set apart as a national deliverer, yet, to avoid offence, he will not undertake the work, till a just and legitimate cause of war occurs."

His parents at first objected to the match, but afterwards went down with him to Timnath, either hoping that something would occur on the way, or when they should arrive, by which they could divert him from his purpose; or they went in his behalf to arrange for the wedding. Substantially this is the manner of conducting such affairs still in the East. Sometimes the proposal is made, however, in a different style. A young fellow says to a father, Such another father will give so much with his daughter; how much will you give if I marry yours? Ordinarily all such negotiations are carried on by the parents of the young people. The leading idea is of bargain and sale. The dower or the purchase money has more influence than the affection of the parties, or their fitness to make each other happy.

As his father and mother were on their way down to

Timnath, Samson goes aside into the vineyards belonging to the town, probably, says Henry, to gather grapes; but another, more poetically inclined, says, Samson wished "to gain the pleasure of a lonely thought." But he had neither the pleasure of a lonely thought, nor of eating grapes, for "a young lion came and roared against him."

I believe this is the first, but certainly not the last time, allusion is made in the Bible to lions. In the subsequent books of the Bible they are frequently mentioned as being found in Palestine and adjacent countries. In the life of David, and in the history of the exploits of his mighty men, they are several times mentioned. On a snowy day one of his worthies killed two lions in a pit. The disobedient prophet was killed by a lion; and the overflowings of the Jordan drove lions from their hiding places in the thickets on its banks. Historically the proof is strong that lions were numerous in ancient times in Asia Minor. They live to be old, and multiply rapidly. It is true, however, that but few, if any, are to be found there at the present time. The monks of Mount Sinai told me in 1851, that lions still prowled through the sandy plains, and over the mountains of the peninsula. But even if not a single lion could now be found in western Asia, the text may be true; for numerous instances can be cited of the disappearing of beasts and plants from countries where they were once numerous. The hippopotamus was once on the lower Nile, but is not there now. The lotus is believed to have been a native of India, but flourished a long time on the Nile, and then disappeared. The slabs, cylinders, walls, columns, and tombs of the ruins of Chaldea, Assyria, and Egypt prove that lions were well known in ancient times. Hunting lions and killing lions is often represented. They are found still on the banks of the Tigris, the Euphrates, and in the Syrian deserts.

There are at least seven Hebrew terms signifying a lion, expressive of the different ages of that animal. *Kephir* in the text, however, signifies a young lion in full strength, and therefore a dangerous adversary. Samson seems not to have been aware of his presence, till the very moment when with open mouth he came fiercely at him ready to devour him. As the lion never roars in the presence of an enemy, except when ready to spring upon him, it is obvious his danger was imminent. The lion roared against him, that is, was about to seize him and tear him to pieces. Samson was now twenty-two years old, but it was not in his own strength that he prevailed over the lion: "The spirit of the Lord came mightily upon him, and he rent him as he would have rent a kid."

That is, supernatural influence excited his body and his mind to an extraordinary degree of energy. As the danger was immediate and extreme, so the divine help was instantaneous. This adventure was singularly prophetic. It was well calculated to inspire him with courage, and to awaken faith in himself and in God. As the king of beasts was as weak as a kid in the sinewy arms of the weaponless hero, and his body soon lay breathless on the ground, so could he with divine assistance overcome the oppressors of his people. It is remarkable that both Samson and David had a lion encounter, as a kind of preparation for their conflict with the Philistines.

"But he told not his father or his mother what he had done." He deemed it best to keep to himself for the present this evidence of God's favour. Perhaps he thought if he told his parents, the Philistines might hear of his great strength, and be more on their guard against him. He judged it best not to arouse their jealousy at present. His modesty and self-control are commendable. In rejoining his parents with as much humility and composure as if he had not performed a great feat, we see the true hero. He was as modest as he was brave. Great talkers, noisy boasters, are seldom good for anything else. Such was Goliah of Gath, but the victory was with the modest son of Jesse.

Hall suggests that if Samson's parents had been behind the hedge witnessing the fight with the lion, they would not have troubled themselves any more about his marriage. They would have concluded his life was lost, for what could an unarmed man do with a lion in his fury? And sure enough, if the tawny adversary had found nothing but a man's strength in his antagonist, it had been an easy victory. "But the spirit of the Lord came upon Samson." And now "if his bones had been brass and his skin plates of iron," it would have been the same thing. He would have rent him as if he had been a kid. The Creator who made the lions stand in awe of Adam, Noah, and Daniel, could easily subdue this one before the giant Hebrew. Let us remember that the most dangerous lion in the way of duty is not the one that springs upon us from the wayside, but the one that lives within us. The strongest lion we have to fight, is the old Adam within.

"Deny thyself, and take thy cross,
Is the Redeemer's great command:
Nature must count her gold but dross,
If she would gain this heavenly land.

The fearful soul that tires and faints,
And walks the ways of God no more,
Is but esteemed almost a saint,
And makes his own destruction sure."

# CHAPTER IX.

## SWEETNESS OUT OF THE STRONG

"But one sad losel soils a name for aye."—*Childe Harold.*

THE fourteenth chapter of Judges opens with an engagement of marriage. We are now going to the wedding, but on our way we have meat out of the eater and sweetness out of the strong. We are now at the beginning of the end. "After a time," Samson returns to take the woman of Timnath to wife. The Hebrew here signifies "after some days," probably after a year. For it was the custom of those days in the East, as it is still, for ten or twelve months to elapse between the betrothment and the marriage. During this time the espoused wife remained with her parents preparing her dresses and ornaments for the wedding. Thus Samson went down with his parents, and the engagement was made, and now he returns to be married. And on his way, as he passes the vineyards where he had killed the lion, he turns aside to see the carcass, and behold it was full of bees and honey. He kept thinking of past providences, although he was on his way to his wedding. The motives that prompted him to turn aside to see the lion's carcass are not stated. But in pondering his ways as he was going to Timnath, it was natural that the sight of the vineyards, where God had delivered him out of the power of the lion, should have excited his gratitude. It was well that a sense of God's goodness revived within him. The dangers we have escaped should not be forgotten. When we are bereaved, we should be careful not to lose the benefits designed by forgetting the hand that afflicts; and when God preserves our friends or raises us up from threatened death, surely thankfulness should fill our hearts. All God's mercies—all his providences to us should be monuments of our gratitude.

1. Some raise a difficulty here by saying that the honey of the ancients was the expressed juice of dates. This may be true of some of their honey, but surely it is not denied that honey bees are as old as Moses. "And he took thereof in his hands," implies according to the original, that he wrested the honey from the bees—that he had to fight with them to get it. And he gave of the honey-comb to his parents; but said nothing to them as to where and how he had obtained it.

2. Some confusion is found in ancient authors about the liking or disliking of bees for dead bodies. A general opinion once prevailed among the heathen that honey bees were generated in carcasses. Virgil is quoted for such an opinion. "But here," says he, "they behold a sudden prodigy, and wondrous to relate, bees, through all the belly, hum amid the putrid bowels of the cattle, pour forth with the fermenting juices from the burst sides, and in immense clouds roll along; then swarm together on the top of a tree, and hang down in a cluster from the bending boughs." Varro is quoted for a directly contrary opinion. He says, "The bee never sits down in an unclean place, or upon anything that emits an unpleasant smell. They are never seen like flies, feeding on blood or flesh; while wasps and hornets all delight in such food, the bee never touches a dead body. So much do they dislike an impure smell, that when one of them dies, the survivors immediately carry out the carcass from the hive, that they may not be annoyed by the effluvia." And

Aristotle says: "The bee will not alight upon a dead carcass, nor taste the flesh."

It is not our business to harmonize Aristotle, Varro, and Virgil, nor to settle the dispute among their learned scholiasts. It may be that these contradictory opinions have arisen from vague traditions concerning Samson's bees. It is a well known historic fact that directly contradictory traditions sometimes flow from one and the same fountain.

But an examination of the text does not decide in favour of either of these theories. It does not say the bees were generated or developed in the lion's carcass. There was "a swarm of bees and honey in the carcass of the lion," but it is not said the bees were hatched there. Nor is it said that the lion had just been killed, or that the flesh was putrid. The contrary is made to appear from the statement, that it was "after a time, he returned." It must have been, as we have shown, about a year after the lion was killed, that the bees were found in its skeleton frame. This was quite time enough, for the birds and beasts of prey to have eaten the flesh off from the bones, and for the hot sun and parching winds of Asia to have completely dried them. Ants and vultures also are very numerous in Asia, and may have helped to prepare the carcass for the bees. The traveller over the plains on the west side of our continent has often seen lying on the road side the bony frame of an ox or of a horse covered with a whole skin, while the flesh was eaten out, or consumed, leaving quite an appropriate place for a hive of bees. Nor are we without evidence of bees having settled themselves in a human skull and in tombs. It is well known that they are very ingenious, and can accommodate themselves to whatever kind of habitation may be at hand wherever they are. Hillocks, crevices of the rocks, and hollow trees and holes in the earth have furnished them hiving places. Jonathan, David's friend, we are told, came upon a bee-hive in the woods, where the honey-comb was dropping from the trees to the ground. 1 Sam. xiv. I fancy the lion's dried frame was a place very much to their liking. It was in a secluded spot, among vines and flowers. And the dry bones saved them a good deal of scaffolding. Herodotus says positively that "bees have swarmed in dry bones." When therefore the caviller at our story has settled his account with the "hoary father of history," then we may have more patience to talk with him about his objections to the natural history of the Bible. The supply of honey was another proof of God's providential interference, and should have taught Samson that God's blessings are often far beyond our expectations. He looked to see the skeleton of the dead lion, and behold it was full of honey.

3. In vindicating Samson from violating his vows in taking honey from the carcass of the lion, we must remember that honey was not a prohibited article. A Nazarite might use it. And then, as we have seen, the lion's carcass was not now foul or unclean. There was no legal pollution in touching the bones of an animal bleached by the winds and rains of twelve months. Honey, says Hall, is honey still, though in a dead lion. And though accidentally met with, and found in a place that was once ceremonially unclean, it was not to be rejected. The grace of God is the more precious if the vessel is unworthy. It is a weak device of the devil to persuade us to neglect the honey, because we do not like the lion. The treasure is in earthen vessels, that the excellence may be of God, and not of man. It is sound theology as well as common sense, to receive and enjoy our heavenly Father's gifts with thankfulness whenever they are bestowed upon us. Honey is not to be despised because it is sweet, nor the light because it is pleasant. Religion does not consist in making every thing sour and bitter. It

is God's will that we should be happy, and rejoice in the use of the good things he gives us. But it is a sin to abuse any of his gifts.

"So his father went down unto the woman: and Samson made there a feast; for so used the young men to do." They are married. The self-will of the young man prevails. His fancy was of more avail than anything else in the universe. Nor are we without similar examples among our every-day sort of people. The ingredients are just the same, only put together in smaller quantities, so that ordinary men are without the characteristic intensity of Samson. They are quite as guilty of earthly passions, but without his heroism. But here is the beginning of the end. Samson married is Samson in trouble. The bane of his life was his fondness for Philistine women. But is this a reflection on God's institution of marriage? Is Samson's unwise choice an argument against wedded life? By no means. The abuse of a good thing does not prove that it is really evil. The marvellous Hebrew is now in bad company. At his wedding

> "He gathered revellers from far and near,
> The heartless parasites of present cheer."

His wife was a heathen. She had not been brought up in the ways of godliness. She had never studied Samson's catechism, nor offered sacrifices to the God of Abraham, as he had done, and as his parents had done before him. There was no community of feeling between them. On every subject there was a want of sympathy. He was a Hebrew, she was a Philistine. He worshipped Jehovah, she worshipped Dagon. In politics and religion they were altogether antagonistic—irreconcilably so. There was no evidence indeed that she had any fancy for him. Her wishes seem not to have been considered at all. Nor does she seem to have had anything to say in the matter. It is strange that Samson should have been so fixed on marrying a woman without any true religion. Piety is woman's highest beauty and greatest protection. A man without religion is bad enough—a poor reprobate without peace; but a woman without religion is still more revolting. She is "a flame without heat; a flower without perfume." Amid all the trials, storms, and tribulations of this world, without religious faith, she is "a drift and a wreck." Who that has ever experienced the sweet truthfulness and abiding love of a godly mother, or a pious wife, or a "sister dear," whose being is in her brother's, and in her devotion to her heavenly Father, can fail to appreciate the worth of piety in woman? Let us have irreligion anywhere else rather than in our mothers, wives, and sisters. They are our guardian angels, and if they become ministers of evil, all men are lost.

It is only where the altars of family worship rise amid the toils of trade and art, and the hearth-stone glows with domestic love, that we expect a permanently prosperous community.

So vastly important is this whole subject—important in a social and patriotic point of view, as well as from a christian stand-point—that I dwell here a little by way of illustration, on the influence of marrying, and of married life in France. And I do so the more, because it has not received the attention, in my humble opinion, that it deserves. The statesman and historian, M. Thiers, in his history of the French Revolution, expresses the belief that the corruptions and troubles of France are to be ascribed to the influence of her women during and subsequent to the reign of Louis XIV. He considers it the great misfortune of France that at the period of the Revolution, all the Bourbons of France, Naples, and Spain were under the influence of their wives and mistresses, who were not the women for their times. It is a curious and highly suggestive fact, that from 1789 to the present time, it has been necessary to reduce the minimum height for enlistment in the troops of the line of France. In 1789 it was five feet one inch French measure. After twenty-five years of constant war—after the battle of Waterloo, the minimum was reduced to less than four feet ten inches; and in 1830, to four feet nine inches. And during the reign of Louis Philippe it was again reduced. And if the same stature of the armies of Louis XVI. were required for the soldiers of Louis Napoleon III., more than one hundred and twenty thousand men would have to be dismissed from the line.

These statements are chiefly taken and abridged from the North British Review for 1857. They are abundantly corroborated, however, by the current reports of France on the subject, and by the English Reviews for the years 1856 and 1857 generally. In the years from 1831 to 1837, 504,000 youths were admitted, and 459,000 rejected from the army of France, because of physical defects. And for the next six years, from 1839 to 1845, the deterioration was even greater—only 486,000 were admitted against 491,000 rejected. As we read history, it is clear that the Copts, Greeks, Italians, and Spaniards as races have deteriorated; while the Germans, the Russians, and the Anglo-Saxons, that is the British, Irish, Scotch, and Americans are still vigorous and advancing in power as nations. But how is it with France? Her emperor at present gives law to Europe. The French are a most extraordinary people. We are prepared to give to them the full meed of fame to which they are entitled. In many things they are emphatically a most wonderful people. But as a nation, their own statistics show they are not advancing in the same ratio, as their neighbours on the continent beyond the Rhine, nor across the channel. At the head of the civilization and political power of the age, how is it that their own army reports show such a marked deterioration in their physical man? I seek not at present any further solution of this question, than to look at it from a moral and religious point of view. And the explanation is found in the words of one of her own great statesmen: France wants religion. Yes, France has consumed her vital energies. She has exhausted herself for glory. Like lands forced to extraordinary fruitfulness, until they are so consumed that even chemical appliances can no longer bring forth the harvest. Wars, and the loss of life and energy, and the consumption of the healthy subsistence of the people by an enormous army, explain in part this exhaustion. But the cause is higher still—lies deeper still. It is found in a disregard of the laws of God in respect to the family. In France the sexual passions are subsidized to science, and licentiousness is governed by a philosophical police; "and in Paris one child in every three is born out of wedlock."

Though the social, martial, and intellectual status of France may at this moment be as high as it ever was, yet her own statistics show an obvious physical deterioration. This deterioration, according to their own army figures, has been going on regularly for almost seventy years. And why? Because the family is not in France what the Bible teaches us it should be. The Bible does not govern the social habits of the French. The Creator, who has the residue of spirits in his hands, and could therefore have created many women for one man, made man male and female. "And wherefore one? That he might seek a godly seed." Mal. ii. 15. The all wise Creator says, also, "It is not good for man to be alone." These ordinances of the Supreme, many of our philosophical neighbours disregard. And if they do not claim that it is good to be alone, they will at least be free from the virtuous ties of the family relation. Our idea of a home they entertain not. They live on the boulevards and in the restaurants. Marriage is either never contracted, or if at all, late in life, and then few children are desired, and even these few are brought up by hired nurses. And the very causes, moreover, that lead to this neglect of marriage, strongly tend to the most pernicious physical results. The unrestrained indulgence of lust and gaiety are so expensive, that a lawful family cannot be supported at the same time; and besides, such indulgences weaken and destroy the constitution. Samson in part illustrates our position. He had no children. If he had married according to the usual custom of his country, and brought up a family, he would have been a far better citizen, a more happy man, and not have come to a violent death.

Politicians and philosophers may affect to smile at our simplicity; but from the lights before us, it is palpable that France in physical stature has deteriorated, while her neighbours of different social habits have not; and in the abuse of the social feelings which the Creator has ordained, and in the want of family organizations on Bible principles, we find causes quite sufficient to explain the diminished stature and physical defects of her masses. The society of women is a necessity of national existence, physically and morally. If "a man discovered America, it was a woman that equipped the voyage." And so it is everywhere. No matter who it is that executes, he was born and trained by a woman. Every Columbus that has left his mark in the world, was furnished by his Isabella mother, who for that purpose laid aside her jewels, it may be her personal comforts, certainly her vanities and time-consuming fashions. Writers on the penal colonies of Great Britain tell us there is but little hope of a female convict unless she marries and becomes a mother. And it is quite as well known that men who are not restrained by the ties of home, and the influence of virtuous women, are almost hopeless. God's laws cannot be improved. Then let the wedded lamp burn brightly and cheerfully where it is already kindled; and if in any of our homes it has grown dim, let it be relumed. And let him be regarded as an enemy to God and man, who discourages marriage and advocates celibacy, or who corrupts society by weakening the bonds of the family which God hath joined together.

## CHAPTER X.

### THE WEDDING RIDDLE AND TRAGEDY.

"Hail, wedded love, mysterious law, true source
Of human offspring, sole propriety
In Paradise of all things common else;
By thee adulterous lust was driven from men,
Among the bestial herds to range: by thee,
Founded in reason, loyal, just, and pure,
Relations dear, and all the charities
Of father, son, and brother first were known.
Perpetual fountain of domestic sweets—
Here love his golden shafts employs, here lights
His constant lamp, and waves his purple wings,
Reigns here and revels; not in the bought smile
Of harlots,—loveless, joyless, unendeared,
Casual fruition; nor in court-amours,
Mixed dance, or wanton mask, or midnight hall,
Or serenade, which the starved lover sings
To his proud fair, best quitted with disdain."

*Milton.*

In the last chapter we went down to Samson's wedding. Let us stay awhile at the feast, and when tired of flowing cups and sparkling wit, we shall have one of those tragedies that marked the earlier administrations of our giant judge. His introduction to the bench was scarcely less distinguished than his exit from it.

"So his father went down unto the woman; and Samson made there a feast; for so used the young men to do. And it came to pass, when they saw him, that they brought thirty companions to be with him."

His father did not go alone; but as the head (Sheikh) of the family, leading them to the wedding, he alone is mentioned. The Chaldaic version has the sense of the passage exactly: "Went down relative to the affair of the woman." The thirty companions, under the pretence of friendship, were really spies. Many of the courtesies of the world, as well as of politicians, are hollow and thankless. "Open defiance is better than false love."

It was the duty of these "children of the bridegroom," as his "friends," to make the company happy. The chief one was called "the governor of the feast," as we see in the marriage in Cana of Galilee. Such was the condition of the Hebrews at this time, that their oppressors would naturally be suspicious of any Hebrew of such noble bearing and prestige as Samson. The Philistines were probably somewhat acquainted with his conduct in the camp of Dan, and would watch him closely, even at his marriage feast.

1. I do not see anything wrong in Samson making a feast, as the young men used to do. It belonged to the bride and her friends to say what its details should be. In so far, then, as he could comply with the customs of her people, without sinning, we find no fault. We may concede prejudices, but cannot compromise a duty. We may surrender our likings, profits, or preferences, but we may not surrender a principle. And I do not see but that it is lawful and proper to conform, in things not sinful, to the customs of those with whom we live. If in the marriage feast there was any recognition of idols, or heathenish ceremonies, then Samson did wrong to submit. Some commentators so understand the history, but I do not see any evidence of idolatrous rites in the marriage or the feast. In teaching us to fear God and keep his commandments, the Bible does

not require us to be proud, mopish, rude, supercilious, or ill behaved. In becoming a christian a man does not cease to be any the less a gentleman. The want of genuine politeness is no proof of true religion.

A careful examination of ancient history is a full verification of the customs alluded to in the text. The Philistines, early Egyptians, and ancient oriental nations, were not Turks in their treatment of women. They were more liberal as to the social position and privileges of their females than modern orientals are. Women, in ancient times, mingled with the men at their feasts, as they do now with us. The monuments of Egypt prove this, as well as the history of the ancient Chaldeans, Persians, Greeks, and Romans. Nor can it be shown, historically, that their presence was a disadvantage—rather the reverse. It has been said by one* of the most observing of men, and withal a great humorist, that "all men who avoid female society have dull perceptions, and are stupid; or have gross tastes, and revolt against what is pure. Your club swaggerers, who are sucking the butts of billiard cues all night, call female society insipid. Poetry is insipid to a yokel; beauty has no charms for a blind man; music does not please a poor beast, who does not know one tune from another. It is better for you to pass an evening, once or twice a week, in a lady's drawing room, even though the conversation is rather slow, and you know the girl's songs by heart, than in a club, tavern, or in the pit of a theatre. All amusements of youth to which women are not admitted, rely on it, are deleterious in their nature." Woman's society is necessary to correct the pride and selfishness of men, for a man is bound to be respectful to a lady. And it is a great point gained for elevating a man's character, and securing

* Thackeray.

his good morals, when he is compelled to feel that there is somebody besides himself whose feelings and tastes are to be consulted—somebody besides his lordly self to whom he must be respectful and attentive. It is well known that men are better behaved, in every respect, when restrained by woman's refining presence.

The same customs alluded to in our history are found still in the East. Islam has not sensibly affected the usages of the Arabs, Turks, Hindoos, Persians, or Africans, except where some peculiar religious rite is concerned. It is not probable that the institutes of Moses made the Hebrews differ from the Canaanite neighbours in their general customs—only where their religion prescribed a difference. Oriental christian women—in Nazareth and Damascus for example—are not distinguished materially from Mohammedan women in their dress and social habits. Women in our mission churches in Mohammedan countries, are separated from the men by a wall or screen when at worship.

2. At weddings it was common to have games, riddles, and the like amusements.

"And Samson said unto them, I will now put forth a riddle unto you: if ye can certainly declare it me, within the seven days of the feast, and find it out, then I will give you thirty sheets and thirty changes of garments. But if ye cannot declare it me, then shall ye give me thirty sheets and thirty changes of garments. And they said unto him, Put forth thy riddle, that we may hear it. And he said unto them, Out of the eater came forth meat, and out of the strong came forth sweetness."

An old scholiast on Aristophanes is quoted by Dr. Clark, as saying that it was "a custom among the ancient Greeks to propose, at their festivals, what were called *griphoi*, riddles, enigmas, or very obscure sayings, both curious and difficult, and to give a recompense to those who found them out, which generally consisted either in a festive crown, or a goblet full of wine. Those who failed to solve them were condemned to drink a large portion of fresh water, or of wine mingled with sea water, which they were compelled to take down at one draught, without drawing their breath, their hands being tied behind their backs. Sometimes they gave the crown to the deity in honour of whom the festival was made; and if none could solve the riddle, the reward was given to him who proposed it."

The classics abound in enigmas proposed at such entertainments. The Greeks excelled in them. The solution of these "banquet-riddles," or "cup-questions," was always highly applauded, and a failure implied a forfeit. Is there any reason why the Greeks did not borrow from Samson's country, by the way of Egypt? And may we not take a profitable lesson from the ancients, as to our social entertainments? It were a much better way to spend our time at seasons of merry-making, in expounding enigmas and riddles, than in slandering our neighbours, or in gluttony or excessive drink. At our weddings let there be entertainment for the mind, as well as employment for the palate and the heels. It is something to avoid all foolish talking and vain jestings, and all filthiness of speech, as an apostle enjoins; but it is more to improve the time for gaining knowledge and strengthening good resolutions. It is surprising how intelligent some men are merely from skill in conversation. They read hardly anything, but from being associated with well informed persons, and being good listeners, and skilful in asking questions, they acquire a vast amount of useful and important information. Our social habits and opportunities should be diligently employed in doing and receiving good.

At the wedding all goes on merrily. Sport and play are

in the ascendant. The cup-questions were as sparkling as the cups. Many were the passages at wit. At last Samson is aroused. He says, I will propose a riddle. He pits his wit against the whole of his companions. If they solve his riddle, he is to pay thirty changes of raiment. If they failed, they are to pay him one change of raiment apiece. The advantages were clearly on their side. They could lose but one change each, while he puts in peril thirty. The strong and the great may afford, however, to be generous, but Samson had an odd humour generally of putting himself against great odds. No doubt he thought himself sure of victory. Nobody but himself knew about the bees and the honey. Why should he not win? The combination of incidents implied in his riddle was certainly rare, if indeed they had ever been found before. But as in all good riddles, the explanation was palpable, beyond dispute, as soon as given. It was like Columbus's solution of making an egg stand on end on the table. As usual on such occasions, as soon as the riddle was propounded, almost every one fancied his ingenuity was competent for the solution. There was much guessing, and many knowing looks among the guests. But the meaning still eluded their grasp. Six days of the seven during which the solution must be given, or the forfeit incurred, have past. Their pride and avarice are excited. They could not brook the idea of being defeated by a young, long-haired, rough looking Hebrew. Nor was it to their taste to part with their fine wardrobes. Nor were they at all scrupulous as to the means they might employ. They were shrewd enough to see in what direction Samson's weakest points lay. Therefore they said unto his wife, "Entice thy husband, that he may declare unto us the riddle, lest we burn thee and thy father's house with fire." The alternative was not a very appropriate one for the honeymoon. It was rather rough language for her countrymen to use if she did not get them out of this difficulty. They do not seem to have had any regard for the innocence of those they were ready to destroy—no regard for human life. It may be that much more may have been said and done than appears from the record. Surely such an appeal would not have been made, even by Philistines, to a young bride, unless the case was deemed a desperate one. Nor can I think, that even a Philistine wife would betray her newly acquired husband in a moment and for a slight cause. Her countrymen must have been very urgent. They must at first have been indignantly repulsed, and have often appealed to her patriotism, and love for her kindred, before she could have entertained their treacherous proposals, and yielded at last under the pressure of their cruel threatenings.

3. The forfeit was thirty sheets and thirty changes of garments. The Hebrew for sheets is *sedinim*, hence the Greek *sindon*, fine linen. The term here means body garments, dresses, shirts rather than sheets—probably garments answering to the *kumja* and *kaftan* of the Arabs. The *kumja* is the shirt that hangs down outside of the drawers to the knees. The *kaftan* is the coat with open sleeves. Others think the sheets of the text are the *chaykes* of the Arabs, answering very nearly to the Scottish highland plaid. The marginal reading *shirts* is in this case the better translation.

"And he went down to Askelon, and slew thirty men of them, and took their spoil, and gave change of garments unto them which expounded the riddle."

"Their spoil," or apparel—the garments they had on, including shirts and cloaks, though not here expressly mentioned. He obtained from them what he needed to pay his forfeit. It may be after all these shirts were the flowing robes of persons of quality. It is highly probable the men whom Samson slew were men of rank, and if such their garments were full and costly. Isaiah uses the same Hebrew term for the splendid dresses of the great in his day. These mantles or shawls, as we should call them, were generally made of wool, though some were made of linen. The young man in the gospel, who followed our Lord, when laid hold of fled naked, leaving "the linen cloth." This does not mean that he was absolutely naked, when he left his plaid. But rather than remain a prisoner, he slipt off his mantle as a man might now do his loose cloak, and ran, leaving it in their hands. A similar explanation belongs to Peter's throwing off his fisher's coat or tunic. The meaning is not that he was in a state of absolute nudity, but deprived of the usual mantle or flowing garment.

4. Let us hear how they proceed with the solution. On the seventh day, the last day of the marriage feast, but not till just before the going down of the sun, they said to Samson, "What is sweeter than honey? and what is stronger than a lion?" In Bible times, in Bible lands, as it is still, it will be remembered that weddings were occasions of great ceremony. The feasting usually continued seven days. Laban, in Gen. xxix. 27, 28, refers to Leah's week of nuptial ceremonies which could not be interrupted by the espousal of Rachel. The Greeks and Romans called the marriage week of feasting "the nuptial joy," and did not allow any work to be done, other than what was necessary to carry on the entertainment, nor permit any signs of mourning. It was also the custom to make and receive presents during the nuptial feast, particularly on the third day. In partriarchal times the bride's father always presented his daughter with a female slave for a handmaid, who was to be inseparable from the family. She was to nurse the mother and the little ones, and to be faithful to her old master's daughter, if all the rest of the world should forsake her. Other presents were also exchanged according to the wealth and rank of the parties, consisting gener-

ally of jewelry, couches, beds, vestments, and all sorts of things reckoned needful for house-keeping.

"And Samson's wife wept before him—wept before him the seven days while the feast lasted." Her weeping was not out of affection for him. Her tears were crocodile tears, or they were tears of terror for her own sake. She loved him not. She said, however, "Thou dost but hate me, and lovest me not: thou hast put forth a riddle unto the children of my people, and hast not told it to me. And he said unto her, Behold, I have not told it my father, nor my mother, and shall I tell it thee?" Is not this the address of a jealous or teasing wife still? When she wishes to have expressions of endearment, does she not hypothecate charges of want of love for her against her husband, that she may have the pleasure of hearing him deny them? Nor is she less skilful than Samson's wife in instituting a rivalry between herself and the children of her own and especially of his people. And is not Samson's answer just the type of an honest heart—of a great and true man? In a simple, straight forward way, he assures her that he had not kept the secret from her from any want of affection. For he had not told it to his own father or mother. Samson's reply is a proverb still in the East. When any one wishes to excuse himself from telling a secret, he says, "Why! I have not told it either to my father or my mother: how then can I tell it to you?" "My friend, do tell me the secret." "Tell you? Yes, when I have told my parents." (See Roberts, and others.) The idea that Samson wished to impress upon his wife was, that he had not treated her with any disrespect or coldness. It is as if he had said: I have been long with my father and mother. They have uniformly treated me with kindness. They have done a great deal for me—much more than I shall ever be able to do for them. They are worthy of my fullest confidence. I love them dearly, and yet I have not told them this secret. How then can I tell it you? If I tell it to you, will I not show a want of respect for them?

I fancy the human races are very much the same in all ages and countries. And although it is heterodox, I should think it about as difficult a thing for a man in modern times to keep a secret as for a woman. I am not sure, but when great interests are involved, women are more trustworthy than men. Their firmness and ready wit in emergencies are proverbial. A Hindoo proverb says: "To a woman tell not a secret." But shall we believe a heathen saying, rather than the experience of a christian age? Samson's heathen wife is not our model. And besides, as it has been shrewdly remarked, if Samson could not keep his own secret, how could he expect his wife to do it? Strange that he was "fool enough to suppose that another would be more faithful to him than he was to himself." Indeed, under all the circumstances, it is wonderful he did not suspect treachery. What just grounds had he to trust in a Philistine woman?

Whether she prevailed, by a promise of secresy or not, the history does not say. If so, the promise was soon broken. It was made to deceive. But who would believe the word of a faithless wife? And yet how can she be resisted? She pleads, and weeps, and accuses him of not loving her. In such a contest, who is always victorious? May not a woman's tears prevail—especially when that woman is a young wife, and the husband uxorious as only Samson could be? Some allowance should be made for the Israelitish judge. Who that ever witnessed a similar strife, can wonder that the strong man did not stand out against her tears? Young, lovely, and his bride! Few men of strong minds would have held out any better than the giant judge. To us his greatest weakness seems to have been his blindness in not seeing the net that was set for him. He must have been one of those honest, simple hearted, unsuspecting great souls that cannot apprehend the depths of the cunning, nor the meanness of the selfish and pusillanimous. And after all, there is a manly, a heroic necessity to rely on the truth and tenderness of woman's nature. In childhood and youth, in manhood and old age, she is man's truest friend. In sickness and sorrow, in works of charity and in acts of piety, she has too often proved herself to be man's angel of mercy, to be traduced by the heartless wretch who is incapable of appreciating her worth. All men are not Samsons, nor are all women like the Timnite bride, nor like Delilah of Sorek. Those who are the loudest and the most profane in their complaints of the weakness of women, are the very men who have themselves done the most to corrupt them. Woman is man's other self—without her he is nothing. She is his blessing and his joy both in the sunshine and beauty of the world, and in its darkness and sorrow. Who, ye revilers of womankind—who were your mothers? And besides, has woman no wrongs—no cruel, outrageous wrongs to avenge, and to avenge only by pouring out to your faithless sex the cup you yourselves have drugged first for her?

5. The solution is given at the appointed hour. Grimly exultant the men of the city, just before the sun went down on the seventh day, said unto Samson: "What is sweeter than honey? and what is stronger than a lion?" In a moment he saw he had been betrayed. "And he said unto them, If ye had not ploughed with my heifer, ye had not found out my riddle." Josephus paraphrases the interview thus: They said to Samson, "Nothing is more disagreeable than a lion to those that light on it, and nothing is sweeter than honey to those that make use of it." To which he replied: "Nothing is more deceitful than a woman; for

such was the perfidious person that discovered my interpretation to you." He meant, doubtless, that without the assistance of his wife, they could not have told the riddle. And on this plea, he might have disputed whether they were entitled to the forfeit. "If ye had not ploughed with my heifer," was probably a common metaphor, or proverb. It seems to have been used with two shades of meaning, one that of licentious intercourse, and the other merely of familiarity. The original does not necessarily convey the idea of wantonness, if it allows it at all. And his return to be reconciled forbids such an interpretation. The idea is this —Samson compares his wife to a young heifer not yet fully subdued to the yoke—not yet learned to go patiently—not yet obedient. This explanation, though it may not be elegant, mitigates her offence, and is fully sustained by the original and the context.

6. Though betrayed and badly treated, Samson scorns to complain, but goes right off to procure the means to pay his forfeit. He was neither a cruel husband nor a repudiator.

"And the Spirit of the Lord came upon him, and he went down to Askelon, and slew thirty men of them, and took their spoil, and gave change of garments unto them which expounded the riddle."

By the Spirit of the Lord coming upon him, we are to understand, that he was inspired with the courage and strength to perform the following feat. He made Askelon his wardrobe, and brought thence the wager of garments for the winning Philistines, lined with the blood of their own countrymen. We know not the causes that led to this pitched battle between Samson and the men of Askelon. Samson may have had a few warriors with him. If he had not, the odds were very great against him. Nor must we forget that the Philistines were at war with Israel. There may have been a nominal truce between Dan and the Philistines of Timnath, and war still raging between the Hebrews and the Askelonites. And we must also remember that in this case, as when Moses slew the Egyptian according to the Noachian precept, Samson was not slaying merely for his own pleasure, nor merely to gratify any personal ill will. He was fulfilling his commission to deliver Israel. The Philistines were idolators—they were enemies to God as well as to him and his countrymen. For their sins they had been already tried in the court of Jehovah, and convicted, and were now under sentence, and Samson was appointed high sheriff to execute the sentence. His acts were therefore by the direction and assistance of God. The Hebrew government in this heroic age was a pure theocracy. Samson was God's lieutenant general, commissioned to execute judgment upon the Philistines. Their crimes were also sins, for Jehovah was both the true God and the acting king of Israel. The punishment on the Philistines was, first, because of their sins against God; yet as God's messenger, the executioner of the divine sentence upon them, Samson was also revenging his own injury and his national wrongs.

As to the hypercriticism urged by some, that as Samson was a Nazarite, he could not have touched the dead bodies to get their garments, it may be answered, that as he was acting under the influence of the Spirit of the Lord, he may have had a dispensation in this case, to do what on ordinary occasions he could not have done, just as our Lord explains the law of the Sabbath; or the prohibition may not have extended to a Nazarite for life, but only for a limited period—or better still, as he was chief magistrate, he could have had no difficulty in obtaining men to strip off their clothes and carry them for him to Timnath.

7. Samson's "anger was kindled and he went up to his father's house." Anger is as natural as a smile. His wife's

treachery was a just cause of anger, and his going up to his father's house at this time showed unusual prudence and forbearance. When he returned to Timnath to pay the forfeit, he seems not to have seen his wife. But lordly as Achilles, and quite as angry and proud in his own self-consciousness of unmerited wrong and impulsive ferocity, he strides off home to his father and mother. It was not wise for him to trust himself in his wife's presence when the sense of his wrongs was so warm within him. He probably feared he might commit some great outrage, if he remained in Timnath. It is to his praise that he thus restrained himself, and that when his anger did burst forth in consuming fire, it was not so much on account of his own wounded pride as to avenge his countrymen. Patriotism and piety are conspicuous in his heroic deeds. And in his lingering at home we see traces of filial love and of early piety. Yet for some reason or other, he does not seem to have made his parents his confidants. He neither told them how he was moved by the Spirit of the Lord, nor did he ask their advice about his plans against their enemies.

"But Samson's wife was given to his companion, whom he had used as his friend." That is, she was given by her father and the chiefs of the town in marriage to his first groomsman. Although she had but little liberty in the matter, still no doubt she was glad the Hebrew was gone, and that she was the wife of his friend. How far Samson was justified in leaving his wife is not altogether clear from the text. Most probably he did not intend a final separation, although this was the result. The whole history is not written out. Many interpreters, inconsistently and strangely, in view of their understanding of the eighteenth verse, blame him as much for leaving his wife as for marrying her. It is a most practical and important matter for us to guard against the demoralization of society by allowing too slight causes to break the nuptial bands. Certainly one of the great sins of our times is the facility of obtaining divorces. Too little sanctity and permanence is attached to the marriage relation. Marriage is a sacred institution. It was a gift from heaven to man before there was any sin. Its purity lies at the foundation of our prosperity. The marriage relation ought not to be dissolved for any slight cause—not from mere whims, or fancies, or momentary passions, nor on account of imaginary wrongs. I could wish our statutes and our practice were more strict on this subject.

The lesson has often been drawn from Samson's marriage—that christians should only marry in the Lord. Samson's case is indeed an admonitory one. Hereditary enemies allied by the most sacred and endearing bonds—a Nazarite, one peculiarly set apart to the service of God, united in matrimony to an idolatress. Speaking after the manner of our times, we should say, a fair face and a warm fancy made sad work with the strongest man's piety. The warning of the good bishop on mixed marriages, although scarcely ever heeded, is worth a repetition. "I wish," says he, "Manoah could speak so loud, that all our Israelites might hear him. Is there never a woman among all thy brethren, or among all thy people, that thou goest to marry a stranger to God and religion?" It were often better to attend our children's funeral than their wedding. Marriage is always a solemn event. Even when the choice has been agreeable to all parties, the future is an unopened volume. A veil of awful mystery hangs before the altar of marriage, which Omnipotence alone can penetrate. There is no surer way to a broken heart, to unutterable woe, and an early grave, than to marry a fool, or a man without correct principles, a sot, a spendthrift, a knave, or a debauchee, though rich as Crœsus, clever as Byron, or handsome as Absalom.

## CHAPTER XI.

### THE JUDGMENT OF THE FOXES.

"And Samson caught three hundred foxes, and took firebrands, and turned tail to tail, and put a firebrand in the midst between the two tails. And when he had set the brands on fire, he let them go into the standing corn of the Philistines, and burnt up both the shocks, and also the standing corn, with the vineyards and olives."

At wheat-harvest, which in Palestine is about the time of Pentecost, when there is much rejoicing in the country, Samson visited his wife with a kid. We have seen that when he was betrayed by his wife, he left her in great disgust, and went to Askelon and slew thirty Philistines and paid his forfeit, and then went home and remained a good while with his parents. In the mean time his anger cools, and his affection begins to return, and not knowing that his wife had been given to his friend, (probably the very person to whom she had revealed the riddle,) he takes a kid, or fawn, and returns to be reconciled to her. His father-in-law was doubtless sincere in offering him his wife's sister in her stead. This was the best indemnity he could make. From the case of Laban, who, after he had cheated Jacob with Leah, gave him Rachel, we see that it was not unusual for a man to marry two sisters. It was probably to correct abuses of this kind that the law of Moses was afterwards enacted. Samson's forbearance is to be noted, as also his effort at reconciliation. Even his purpose to avenge himself, seems to be the utterance of a patriotic judge, rather than of an aggrieved husband. If he had meditated retaliation merely for his personal injuries, his wife and her father were the parties to have been chastised. But he felt that it was as an Israelite chiefly that he had been injured, and as such he would be more guilty than even the Philistines, if he did not avenge this national insult. His manner of avenging himself was extraordinary, singular, and effective. His agents were one hundred and fifty pairs of foxes, with firebrands tied to their tails, which burned their corn, and vineyards, and olives. In the time of wheat-harvest, the corn was partly standing, and partly gathered into shocks; all dead ripe, and of course easily burned. Infidels have attempted to be merry over Samson's foxes and the burning cornfields of the Philistines. But let such remember that the corn was not maize or Indian corn, but wheat, which when ripe could be easily burned, either standing in the field or gathered into shocks. And as to Samson's ability to catch so many foxes, let it be observed:

1. That the Hebrew *shualim* may comprehend not only foxes, but wolves and hyenas. The Bible name for fox is supposed to be derived from its habit of burrowing or dwelling in holes in the earth, and may be as applicable to wolves, hyenas, and jackals as to foxes. The Septuagint and the Vulgate both understand the animal in this place to be the fox. It is true that a different Hebrew word is used for the jackal; but it is probable the term *shualim* included this animal also. Hasselquist and some other naturalists have thought the *shual* of Palestine was an animal between a wolf and a fox—"the little eastern fox," as they denominate it, and not our ordinary fox. When hungry, this animal is said to devour little children, and even old and

feeble persons. It is only by the context that we can tell what kind of animals are meant in a given passage.

2. But taking the term here in its comprehensive sense, as we well may, there is no doubt but that the country was full of foxes. The Scriptures often speak of them in the Holy Land. Their cubs ruined the vineyards, according to the Song of Solomon, ii. 15. "Take us the foxes, the little foxes that spoil our vines." And Jeremiah laments that the foxes had taken possession of the hills of Judea. Lam. v. 18. And Ezekiel compares the numerous false prophets of his day to the same animals, xiii. 4. And in the first book of Samuel, a portion of this very country is called Shual, that is the land of foxes—famous for the number of these animals found in it. And a neighbouring city belonging to one of the tribes of Israel was called Hazar-shual; that is, the abode or habitation of the fox. Every traveller through the country to this day, confirms the testimony of Bochart, Bellonius, and Morizon, that it swarms with animals of this species. They lurk in companies of two or three hundred on the borders of the desert, and in the ruins of old towns, and in the ledges of the rocks.

3. Samson was no doubt an expert hunter as well as a terrible fighter, and well skilled in taking foxes. And then, as a chief magistrate, he could have employed as many men to assist him as was necessary. When Nebuchadnezzar is said to have built the great Babylon, and Solomon to have built the temple at Jerusalem, the meaning is not that they did all the work with their own royal hands. They did not lay a single brick, stone, or timber themselves. But they caused the work to be done. There is no necessity then to prove that Samson caught all the foxes himself. Nor,

4. Are we restricted to any short or definite period of

time in which the foxes must have been taken. It is not said they were all caught in one hour, one day, or one week. He may have been several months in capturing them, for anything the text says.

5. Some say, though I do not attach any importance to the suggestion, that a miraculous agency was employed in bringing the animals to Samson, as in causing them to come to Adam to be named, and to Noah into the ark. It is not denied that God can control the instincts and guide the propensities of beasts, birds, and fishes. This we see in Daniel's lions, Noah's dove, and Peter's fish; but when there was no necessity, so to speak, for divine interposition in a miraculous manner, I prefer not to call for it. In theology, as in philosophy, there is no useless expenditure of Omnipotent energy. But a miracle is none the less a true miracle, because the means by which it is wrought are natural. The converging of the natural agencies in force on the desired point and for an avowed purpose, is sufficient to make a miracle.

Surely it is not so unheard of and incredible a thing, to have collected such a number of these animals in ancient times, as to destroy the credibility and literality of our story, because it contains this statement about the foxes. Did not Sylla show at one time to the Romans one hundred lions? And Cæsar four hundred, and Pompey six hundred? The history of Roman pleasures, according to the books, states that the Emperor Probus let loose into the theatre at one time one thousand wild boars, one thousand does, one thousand ostriches, one thousand stags, and a countless multitude of other wild animals. At another time he exhibited one hundred leopards from Libya, one hundred from Syria, and three hundred bears. When the caviller settles his hypercriticism with Vopiscus's Life of Probus, and with Roman history generally, we shall then consider whether our story should be rejected as incredible because of its three hundred foxes.

It has also been proved by learned men that the Romans had a custom, which they seem to have borrowed from the Phenicians, who were near neighbours of the Philistines—if they were not Philistines themselves—of letting loose, in the middle of April, (the feast of Ceres)—the very time of wheat-harvest in Palestine, but not in Italy—in the circus, a large number of foxes with burning torches to their tails. Is Samson's the original, or did he adopt a common custom of the country? The story of the celebrated Roman vulpinaria, or feast of the foxes, as told by Ovid and others, bears a remarkable similarity to the history before us, ascribing the origin of this Roman custom to the following circumstance: A lad caught a fox which had stolen many fowls, and having enveloped his body with straw, set it on fire and let him run loose. The fox, hoping to escape from the fire, took to the thick standing corn which was then ready for the sickle; and the wind blowing hard at the time, the flames soon consumed the crop. And from this circumstance ever afterwards, a law of the city of Rome required that every fox caught should be burnt alive. This is the substance of the Roman story, which Bochart and others insist took its rise from the burning of the cornfields of the Philistines by Samson's foxes. The Judean origin of the custom is certainly the most probable, and in every way the most satisfactory. Commemorative institutions or fêtes always have their origin in facts. Of this we may be well assured, though the record of the original facts and even the facts themselves should be lost through the lapse of time. (See Ovid and his Scholiasts. Fastor. lib. iv. vers. 679.)

"And took fire-brands." Our word *lamp* is probably through the Greek *lampas*, from the Hebrew original in this place, *lapidim*, or, as it is in the Chaldee and Syriac, *lampidim*. These *lampidim* were a kind of torch or flambeau, made with pitch. The animals seemed to be tied together in pairs, tail to tail, by cords of moderate length, and the torch fastened to this cord about midway. How

these animals thus treated would act, we may easily comprehend. It is well known that the whole fox race is prone to range about houses and fields, and when frightened, as these were, to run for cover to the thickest corn, if standing, or for the sheaves or stacks, if gathered; and being vexed by the pain of the fire, they would first worry, and snap, and fight, and run at cross purposes, and so spread the conflagration, until we are quite ready to conclude with Calmet, "that nothing could be better adapted to produce a general conflagration, than this expedient of combustion-communicating jackals. We must therefore suppose these torches were at some distance from the animals, so as not to burn them, and that they burnt long without being consumed."

I am not aware that any experiment has ever been made to see how foxes would act tied tail to tail with a fire-brand between them. But Dr. Kitto, (to whose Biblical Illustrations I would especially refer the reader for much valuable information on this and kindred topics,) says he once saw two dogs so tied together, and that they first pulled in contrary directions, and made no head way at all; but at last ran off parallel with considerable speed. And it is presumed foxes are as sagacious as dogs. At first there may have been some indecision and uncertain turnings, but very soon each couple found that the only way to reach cover, was for them to run together in parallel lines distant from each other by the length of their tails and burning brands. And thus the very purpose was all the more effectually carried out. The fox is a swift runner. And when tied together as in this case, they were sure to run this way and that way, and to spread the fire all over the fields. Nor could they readily escape to the woods, or to their holes in the rocks, where the fire-brands would have been extinguished.

It will be remembered that the cornfields of that country were not separated by high fences, or deep ditches or hedges, but extended as now in Celo-Syria, or Esdraelon, as far as the eye can see, one vast level unbroken plain of waving grain. One hundred and fifty pairs of such animals, running with flaming torches to their tails, would very soon set an immense plain in a blaze. The tying of the animals in pairs may have been to prevent their reaching cover too soon. And besides, if the fire brand had been attached to them singly, the tail would have fallen to the ground, and the brand would have soon died out; but being sustained by the tension between the pair, the brand flamed out, and burnt all the better for their rapid motion after it was once kindled, and so the greater would be the damage.

Frequent fires occur to this day among the towns of the interior of Asia and Africa, that are kindled and made to spread from town to town by their enemies tying a burning cotton thread to the tail of a large species of buzzard, which flies to the thatch of the houses when set adrift.*

Dr. Kitto says of the burning of the harvest-fields, that as bread is the staff of life, if any other man than Samson had done it, he should have been "hanged"—"that it looks like both a religious and social sacrifice, deliberately to waste and destroy it." Now if it would have been right to hang any other man for doing what Samson did under the same circumstances, then Samson should have been hanged. But where is the authority for hanging or taking away life for any crime except that of murder? And besides, I do not see the affair in that light. Was not Samson the divinely commissioned deliverer of Israel? Were not the Philistines at war with Israel? Had he not then a right to cut off their supplies? It is allowed in war to deprive an enemy of the means of subsistence, and thus liberate the state from their depredations. But if this is not sufficient, our hero bore a divine commission before he was born, to do the Philistines all the harm he could. This must end the strife. The method adopted we have admitted was a singular one, but it was very effective. Samson's commission was to deliver Israel from the Philistines. He was raised up to be a judge, called and appointed by God himself, who was then the only king of Israel, to execute judgment on the Philistines. He was not acting as a private person, nor taking the law into his own hands, nor assuming the sovereignty of the state. It was his duty to prosecute the mission for which God had raised him up. True, he is now the more ready to begin it, because he has personal wrongs to avenge. But he feels that it is as an Israelite that he has been insulted and wronged in the matter of his wife, and his patriotism and the honour of his God

* Capt. Clapperton's Journal of his Second Expedition, p. 274.

require him to punish them. His enemies are numerous and more warlike than his own countrymen. Their fields are full of ripe corn. The country abounds in foxes. These animals are swift runners. Why may he not use them as his agents in afflicting the Philistines? Why may he not rid the country of so many of these noxious animals either by thus destroying them, or frightening them away, and at the same time avenge his personal wrongs by punishing the Philistines in the way that would bring upon them the highest ridicule and contempt?

In this history we have a most remarkable illustration of the terrible law of retribution which the Supreme Ruler of the universe has ordained, the presence of which runs like a flame of fire through all the history and through all the dispensations of providence. In selecting foxes as instruments of his vengeance, Samson selected the animals which, of all others, were the most appropriate to the nature of the insult. Foxes are cunning; and it was through their wit the Philistines had prevailed against him. They had won the garments by stratagem, and now their cornfields are burned by foxes.

But the judgments of God that begin on a man's property, if not arrested by penitence and forgiveness, soon take hold of his person. This was the process even with Job, and with the Egyptians, though in them the attributes illusstrated are different. From the murrain among their cattle, the Lord proceeds until the first born is slain. "And if judgment begin at the house of God, what will be the end of the ungodly, who obey not the gospel?"

When the Philistines saw their cornfields, vineyards, and olive-yards destroyed, they at once understood how and for what it was done; they therefore came and burnt Samson's wife and her father, inflicting upon her the very death threatened, and to escape which she had betrayed her newly married husband. Because Samson had burnt their fields of corn, the Philistines burnt the Timnites. They must have felt that Samson had been unjustly treated, and hoped by this means to appease him. The retribution upon Samson's wife and father was most inhuman and barbarous, and in every way out of all proportion in its severity. It does not appear that either of them had any thing to do with the burning of the cornfields, yet their own countrymen burn them for what the Hebrew Samson had done. The fire-brands of the running foxes were not so destructive as the fire of dissension kindled among the Philistines. There is nothing more pleasing to the enemies of free institutions than to see their friends pulling each other by the ears. No other hands but our own can ever pull down and destroy the temples of justice, liberty, and religion erected for us by our blessed fathers in this fair land. Union is our strength.

Samson's wife in trying to avoid Scylla fell into Charybdis. She betrayed her husband, because she feared her brethren would burn her and her father's house with fire, and yet by their hands she was burned with fire and her father also. She leaped into the flames she meant to avoid. The Jews who crucified our Lord did just the same thing. They professed to proceed against him to put him to death as Cæsar's friends, lest the Romans should come and destroy them. And they succeeded in crucifying him, but the Romans came, and burnt their temple and city with fire. It is still the rule of providence, that as men measure to others so it shall be measured to them again. It should be eternally before our minds, that *true principle is the only expediency.* What God does is right. What he commands we must do. His will is the supreme rule. Our duty is obedience. All history, both sacred and profane, shows that the evil that men do in trying to escape by continuing to sin—by doing wrong to correct a wrong—by doing evil that good may come, even when their motives are admitted to be good—always meets them sooner or later in their flight. Sin added to sin only enhances guilt. The history of the dishonest and the licentious is an illustrated commentary on this rule Those that hasten to be rich, by resorting to dishonest means, and have accumulated property by fraud, do not generally long enjoy it. They seldom retain their gains, and if they do, how can they enjoy them haunted with a guilty conscience? The general rule is, that Haman himself hangs on his own gallows, and not Mordecai. It is a singular and significant providence that so many of the inventors of means for taking the life of their fellow men, should have perished by their own inventions. Gunpowder was the death of its inventor; Phalaris was destroyed by his own "brazen bull." The regent Morton who first introduced the "Maiden," a Scottish instrument of decapitation, like the inventor of the Guillotine, perished by his own instrument. The same is true of Brodie, who induced the Edinburgh magistrates to use the "new drop," the same still in use. Marat, the bloody-minded, died from the assassin's dagger. Danton and Robespierre conspired the death of Vergniaud and of his republican confreres, the noble Girondists, and then Robespierre lived only long enough to see the death of Danton before perishing himself by the same guillotine. The duke of Orleans, the infamous Egalité, voted for the death of Louis XVI, and not long afterwards was guillotined himself. The wicked are taken in their own net. They fall into the ditch their own hands have digged. "Bloody minded and deceitful men shall not live out half their days." Sinning is a sure paymaster, and if delayed, the interest compounds rapidly. It is not necessary to adjourn to the court of futurity to know that sin is an evil thing and bitter. The way of the transgressors against both natural and moral laws is *now* hard. The day of reckoning follows hard after sinful indulgence. Nature is inexorable. Her outraged laws must be avenged. The libertine and the drunkard find it to be so. Their bodies and minds soon bear the marks of guilt and punishment. Passions and appetites abused soon change the body into a prison for the soul. No fugitive escapes the police of God and nature. The penalties annexed by the Creator to the violation of the laws of our physical constitution, are as awful as they are inevitable. Sooner or later, at home or abroad, on land or sea, conscience will awake and seize the guilty; and abused nature will cry out, and fearful retribution will fall upon them; or if not in this life, it will be all the more fearful because it falls upon them beyond the grave, where no repentance nor acts of pardon are known. But this is the day of grace. This is the hour of pardon. There is a great Redeemer, the Lamb of God, who taketh away the sin of the world. And if we confess our sins to God, he is faithful and just to forgive us our sins, and to cleanse us from all unrighteousness. "The blood of Jesus Christ his Son cleanseth us from all sin."

# CHAPTER XII.

## THE JAW-BONE SLAUGHTER.

——"My life hath been a combat,
And every thought a wound, till I am scarr'd
In the immortal part of me."—*Manfred.*

"AND Samson said unto them, Though ye have done this, yet will I be avenged of you, and after that I will cease. And he smote them hip and thigh with a great slaughter. And he went down and dwelt in the top of the rock Etam." The reader will please read the fifteenth chapter of Judges from the seventh verse to the end. Homer's heroes were never at a loss for weapons, for with whatever kind of arms they began to fight, they always finished by throwing stones. The "fierce Tydides" scrupled not to throw a rocky fragment so great that two men in the degenerate days of the poet could not raise it against a foe; and

"Where to the hip the inserted thigh unites,
Full on the bone the pointed marble lights;
Through both the tendons broke the rugged stone,
And stripped the skin and crack'd the solid bone."
*Iliad, Lib. v.* 375—378.

The traveller from Thun to Grindelwald in the Bernese Alps, is shown to this day the huge stones with which the Swiss Samsons have been wont to amuse themselves. They are not so large, it is true, as the mountains which the giants are fabled to have plucked up and used as javelins in their wars; but they are of enormous size.

The learned give various explanations of this "hip and thigh" slaughter. Good critics say that the text literally means, that in their running away from Samson, he kicked them down, and then trod them to death; and thus his leg or thigh was against their hip. Gesenius considers the phrase as a proverbial expression, meaning that he smote them with a great slaughter, cutting them all to pieces and scattering their limbs promiscuously, literally, "leg upon thigh." It was certainly a most extraordinary battle. One, and he unarmed, contending with many thousands, and these thousands covered with armour and fighting with their chosen weapons. But it is probable the fear of the Lord fell on them as soon as Samson began to deal his terrific blows, so that in their panic they trampled down, and bruised, and rendered unfit for service even a greater number than were killed outright. Though translators differ as to the application of some of the words found in this passage, all agree in the general meaning. Proverbial phrases are always hard to explain, after the language in which they have their origin ceases to be a living tongue.

It is much more important to notice the principle on which Samson acted, than to explain how he smote them. The history of this fight is brief. We are not told how, nor on what account they met. Generally Samson's movements against the Philistines were aggressive; but here, I think, they attacked him. No doubt they were always ready for any opportunity to seize his person, or to kill him. But when they came upon him, he slew them "hip and thigh with a great slaughter." He was not acting as a mere private person, even if he were entirely alone. He was the chief magistrate, and commissioned from heaven to execute divine sentence upon the Philistines.

"And he dwelt in the top of the rock Etam." From 1 Chron. iv. 3, 33, and 2 Chron. xi. 6, it would seem that Rehoboam built a fortress, or fortified a town near the rock Etam, which was called by the same name. This place was within the territory of Judah, between Tekoah and Bethlehem. And according to Josephus, who calls it Hethan, it was fifteen miles from Jerusalem. The rock probably gave name to the town, and was famous for its natural strength, or safety as a place of retreat. David sought refuge often in the caves of Engedi, (Ain Jiddy). The strongholds of the hill country of Judea, were its caves and holes in the rocks. 1 Sam. xxiii. and xxiv.

In the military operations of the French in Africa a few years since, a number of Arabs took shelter in a rock cavern, and so ably defended themselves, that they had at last to be destroyed by making a fire in the cave's mouth. In 1634 when the Sultan ordered the Bashaw of Damascus to make the rebel Emir Faccardine a prisoner, the latter shut himself up in the hollow of a great rock, with a small number of his officers. The Bashaw besieged him several months, but at last when he had made all necessary preparations to blow up the rock, the Emir surrendered.

From the twentieth verse—"And he judged Israel in the days of the Philistines twenty years,"—it is to be inferred that during all his administration the Philistines were troublesome. It was his mission only to begin the deliverance of his people. The Philistines were harassed and weakened, but not wholly overcome. Their yoke was not broken till the days of David.

While Samson is in the cave of the rock Etam his countrymen appear to have been in a very humiliating condition. We have found that at a subsequent period they were inferior to the Philistines as manufacturers, and obliged to go to them to get their axes and coulters sharpened. They appear here inferior also as warriors, and except when led by some champion under miraculous impulses, they were not able to stand before them in battle. From the confession of the men of Judah in the eleventh verse, it is clear their spirit was broken, and their heart was as water. Their only desire was to escape farther annoyance from the Philistines by making Samson their prisoner. They were more anxious to sacrifice him to their enemies, than to follow him in a glorious struggle to victory or death. After the evidence they had of his power to deliver them, their pusillanimity seems almost incredible.

"Why are ye come up against us?" said the men of Judah to the Philistines. We pay our tribute punctually: we have committed no new offence. True, said the lordly Philistines; we have no new cause of complaint against you. But there is a Hebrew harboured among you, or dwelling in your territory, who has done us a great deal of mischief. "To bind Samson are we come up, to do to him, as he hath done to us." And then the men of Judah, three thousand strong, went up to the top of the rock Etam to bind Samson, to deliver him into the hands of the Philistines Shame, ye men of Judah! Why did you not rather put your giant judge, Jehovah's lieutenant-general, at the head of your forces, and strike a blow for God and liberty? And they said to Samson, Do you not know that we are under the yoke of the Philistines, and that we are not able to shake it off? Why then are you continually insulting and provoking them? Do you not know that we must smart for all your provocations? But now mark the hero's reply. He speaks with becoming magnanimity. He does not upbraid them, as he might very justly have done, for their want of honour and courage; but generously forbearing all reproach, stipu lates only that they shall not lay hands on him themselves. I have done to them, says Samson, only as they have done unto me. But swear unto me, that ye will not fall upon me yourselves, and you may bind me, and deliver me into their hands.

Samson must have been strongly posted to render it necessary for so large a force to come to take him, or they must have had a most extraordinary idea of his strength and courage. It is a mooted point with commentators whether he had a body guard of tried men, or was alone. I should think from the nature of his office, and from this whole history, that he was alone, and without any warrior band. But I see no reason why he could not have delivered himself from the men of Judah, as easily as he did soon afterwards from the Philistines, except that he had no divine commission to kill his countrymen. Nor is there any evidence that he had any wish ever to imbrue his hands in their blood. His mission was specific. Nor can I find any justifiable excuse for his cousins the men of Judah. The Philistines were their oppressors. They were the enemies of their fathers and of their religion. God had raised up Samson to be a deliverer. Why then did they not now strike for their altars and their sires, their wives and their little ones? Instead of this, with craven heart, they bind their God-sent champion, who voluntarily surrenders himself to them, to deliver him into the hands of the Philistines. It was nothing that Samson was not of their tribe. He was a Hebrew. It was nothing that Washington was of Virginia rather than of Massachusetts. He was an American. And we, though of different states, are all Americans. We have one father, one constitution, and one destiny.

In the stipulation also that they would not fall upon him themselves, there is still greater shame. I am painfully aware that some excuses are alleged for their not rallying to his standard that are not altogether groundless. It is said, that Samson was not really a fit leader, because his intellect was weak and his character sadly inconsistent. Though of gigantic physical strength, his character was not well balanced. But was his intellect weak in the inverse ratio that his body was strong? Now even if we admit that such is the ordinary law of mankind, it does not follow that it must have been true in his case. For, as has already been remarked, Samson does not appear to have been of gigantic stature, nor to have had gigantic strength, except when the Spirit of the Lord moved him. That he was naturally strong and of powerful muscle, we admit; but his great strength was miraculous. It could not therefore have impaired his mind on the principle suggested above. It is true that great physical powers are sometimes possessed by those who have but little mental energy, and less moral character; but has any law of nature been discovered making a large man or a strong man a bad man? If a strong body must be the dwelling of a weak mind, we have been erroneously taught—that the perfect man is a sound mind in a sound body. We admit that Samson's mental energy and moral sense strike us as dwarfish in comparison with his great bodily strength. Not to such a degree, however, as to excuse the men of Judah for not trusting in him as God's agent. Though a strong man, Samson was not a truly great man. Speaking from our starting point of his history, we should say his attacks upon the Philistines were badly planned, and the results wholly insignificant. He was a man sadly wanting in self-control, mental discipline, and refinement of conscience. His two great passions were love and revenge, and both always directed towards the same people, and both badly managed. He seems to have done nothing towards the accomplishment of his great mission, except when under some supernatural impulse. The victories of Barak, Gideon.

and Jephthah near his own time, were of more enduring brilliancy and effect. The fact is Samson was not the man he ought to have been. He suffered his sensuality to mar his otherwise greatness of character. His own countrymen did not rally to his standard. They had not confidence in him. His character was so spasmodic, he acted so by fits and starts, that they distrusted his prudence. And are they much to be blamed for withholding their confidence from a man who was so often the slave of his own senses? A pretty face or a few tears were quite enough to unman him. He was a teetotaler in one way, but very intemperate in another. If wine did not ruin him, women did. The elders of Judah and the warriors of his own tribe might then well hesitate to risk their fortunes and lives under the command of one, who could repeatedly sacrifice the most important interests to a woman's sighs, and reveal his holy secret at the importunities of a paramour.

The utter worthlessness of the two new cords is very strongly expressed in the original. "His bands loosed;" that is, melted from his hands. "They became as flax that was burnt with fire." That is, they were like flaxen ropes burnt, still retaining their coil and shape, but without strength; mere cinders which, as soon as touched, fall to pieces. So worthless were the two new cords with which they bound Samson fast, when the Spirit of the Lord came mightily upon him.

Listen now to the savage yells of the Philistine hosts, as they saw the great Hebrew bound and coming to them from the rock from which they were not able to fetch him. But their shout was his signal for action. Rending the new cords as burnt flax, "he found a new jaw-bone of an ass, and put forth his hand and took it, and slew a thousand men therewith." The *new* of the text is applied by some not to the jaw-bone, but to the carcass, and rendered *tabid* or *putrid*.

If so, then the idea is, that the body being in a putrid state, he could the more easily separate the bone from the integuments, and thus procure such a bone as would be most fit for execution. But if the term new is applied to the body, it is also true of the jaw-bone, and its being new was of importance, for it was therefore heavy and tough. It would bear harder blows without breaking. And never was there a more terrible weapon than this jaw-bone in Samson's hand. Never did an ass's jaw-bone do such service since the foundation of the world.

The sixteenth verse is Samson's pean, or hymn of triumph. Though rather a silent man, and heretofore as modest as brave, there is nothing censurable in his singing after the manner of his times a stanza, in commemoration of his own exploits.

> "With the jaw-bone of an ass, heaps upon heaps,
> With the jaw of an ass have I slain a thousand men."

The beauty and force of this verse can hardly be appreciated without a knowledge of the original, where we have a paranomasia on the identity of the terms for *ass* and a *heap*. The point seems to be in Samson's saying, that the Philistines fell under his blows with the jaw-bone of an ass, as tamely as if they themselves had been stupid asses—"heaps upon heaps."

"A thousand" here is not necessarily to be understood as a definite number, but denoting a great many. The young women, in singing David's praises when he came as "the conquering hero" from the killing of Goliah, said, he hath slain his "tens of thousands," when in fact He had killed but one person. He was, it is true, a giant, who was worth ten thousand common Philistines. To have slain so many with a Damascus blade would have been a prodigious feat; what then shall we say of its being done with the jaw-bone of an ass? No doubt, fear helped him. The Philistines seeing Samson's cords broken, remembering what he had done at Askelon, and struck with terror at the tremendous execution of his giant arm, and expecting that now all the armed thousands of Judah would join him, and that they would all be dead men, fled, and in their disorderly flight many of them were killed. The victory, however, was not in the weapon, nor in Samson's arm, nor because of the Philistines' terror. It was God that nerved his heart and strengthened his arm. The armed men of Judah could have furnished Samson with a sword; but greater contempt was cast upon these idolators by laying them "heaps upon heaps" with a jaw-bone.

"And called that place Ramath-Lehi." Twice before it is called Lehi by anticipation. Lehi was used for brevity's sake. Such contractions were common with Hebrew proper names. Jerusalem was called also Salem. Ramath-Lehi means "the hill of the jaw-bone," or "the casting away of the jaw-bone." For here he cast away the jaw-bone out of his hand. Samson was not a good collector of relics. That jaw-bone would be a fortune in our day.

The excessive thirst of which he expected to die, or to be obliged to surrender to the Philistines, was the natural consequence of excessive fatigue. Josephus thinks this dreadful thirst was brought on him for his pride, in not acknowledging God in his triumphal song. "Heaps upon heaps, I have slain a thousand men," said he; but not a word of praise to Jehovah for helping him. God was not recognized in the affair at all. Like Nebuchadnezzer, saying, "Is not this great Babylon that I have built?" And the judgment of God fell on him from heaven till he was humbled to acknowledge the sovereignty of the Most High. Whether this is the proper explanation of Samson's thirst or not, pride is a great sin, and high looks are an abomination to the Lord.

"But God clave a hollow place that was in the jaw-bone, and there came water thereout." Here is an error in our translation. The fountain of water was not in the jaw-bone. The mistake of our translators, who are generally so correct, was doubtless made in this way: The same Hebrew word is rendered both *Lehi*, a proper name, and also *jaw-bone*. The mistake therefore was in confounding the name of the place for the instrument of the victory from which the place derived its name. The meaning is, God clave a hollow place of the rock or earth at Lehi, and a fountain gushed forth and continued to flow up to the time of the writing of the history. And in memory of the deliverance, the fountain was called En-hak-kore, that is, "the well of him that cried;" "Invocation well." Tradition still points out the stream that gushed from the grotto of Lehi for the refreshing of the Hebrew warrior.

We close this chapter with a lesson from the shouting of the Philistines on the eve of their terrible slaughter. Their defiant shout was the knell of their complete overthrow. And it is still true that "a dreadful sound is in the ears" of the wicked: "in prosperity the destroyer shall come upon him." Job xv. 21. The triumphing of the ungodly is short. Their prosperity is their destruction. Had there been as many devils as there were Philistines, when the Spirit of the Lord came upon Samson, he would have turned their shoutings into wailings quite as easily. Never are the ungodly more to be pitied than when their prospects seem to be the brightest. Their fancied security is their ruin. We are told that more vessels are lost in a fair gale than in tempests. Nothing is so much to be feared as a sinner's apparent peace. Present impunity does not argue the abatement of the divine wrath.

The delays of providence do not change the nature of sin. It remains intrinsically the abominable thing that God hates. In the very nature of things it is impossible that sin should any where or at any time meet with his approbation. The patience of God does not therefore imply any mitigation of the enormity of wrong-doing. It is no proof of divine indifference to sin, that God does not instantly express his abhorrence of it, and pour out his wrath upon the offender. Men may kindle immediately into a transport of passion when insulted; but God is not a man, and therefore we are not consumed. He punishes sin, not from passion, but from principle—not to avenge himself for any injury he sustains from sin, but in order to maintain a righteous government:—such a government as is necessary for the happiness of his creatures. Such an administration is also agreeable to his infinite holiness. And the punishment of sin will only be the more severe, because of the aggravations of abused mercy. Delay in a human government may lessen the certainty of punishment, by leaving room for escape, or for the loss of opportunity or ability for inflicting the punishment; but it is never so with God. "One day is with the Lord as a thousand years, and a thousand years as one day." There is, then, no statute of limitation within which process against the sinner must begin, or within which his cause must be tried and the sentence executed. Nay, though the final sentence against an evil work is sometimes delayed, and therefore the hearts of men are more fully set to evil, still the accusation begins in most cases immediately. Conscience speaks out. Violated laws plead against the transgressor, and his ways are found to be hard. Evil doing is itself a judgment. And the delay to execute the sentence against evil doing is sometimes a part of the sentence. The delay, if not improved, is not a blessing. As in divine mercies, the rule is "grace upon grace," one favour received thankfully, drawing another; so it is with punishments; if not improved—one stroke draws down another. It were often a great mercy to arrest the guilty in their career of crime. There is something awful in being given over to blindness of mind and hardness of heart, to treasure up wrath against the day of wrath, by abusing the long-suffering, and patience, and goodness of God. The men of Judah were restrained from laying their hands upon Samson. And the Philistines, in shouting for joy at his surrender, were not able to touch him. Wicked men are often not so bad as they would be, if they were not restrained. They are not more cruel, simply because they cannot be. Even in Samson's forbearance towards his own countrymen, there was a divine hand. He was sent against the Philistines, and would not therefore touch his spiritless countrymen. Oh that men would remember that a thing is not good simply because it seems to prosper, but because it is according to the will of God! That only is right which God commands. Sin is evil, not because it is punished, but because it is disobedience—it is something forbidden. Any delay, therefore, of sentence against evil doers, instead of encouraging them to continue in sin, should melt them to penitential sorrow. Instead of lulling them into security, it ought to alarm them. Nothing but pardon secures their safety. No length of time, nor flight, nor distance from the place of sinning can give any true relief. Nothing but pardon can save the sinner. He must be forgiven, or sink to endless perdition. But there is forgiveness with God, that he may be feared. He that confesseth and forsaketh his sins shall find mercy.

# CHAPTER XIII.

## THE DREADFUL RELAPSE FROM ETAM.

"But what availed this temperance, not complete,
Against another object more enticing?
What boots it at one gate to make defence,
And at another to let in the foe?—*Samson Agonistes.*

IN the first three verses of the sixteenth chapter of Judges, we have a brief account of Samson's visit to Gaza, and of what befel him there. "Then went Samson to Gaza," a city about sixty miles southwest from Jerusalem, and only a few miles from Askelon. It was one of the oldest cities in the world, and is always represented in the Old Testament as a place of considerable importance. It was once a city of great wealth. The present town is beautifully situated on a hill, amidst gardens of olive and date trees. The houses are mostly of stone, but its inhabitants are poor. Its chief articles of trade are cotton and soap.

The Hebrew term *zonah*, and its corresponding one in Greek, *porne*, which is applied to the woman of Gaza, is a word of uncertain signification. Our word harlot is not a word of doubtful meaning, but the Hebrew *zonah* is not always its equivalent. There is nothing in the history of Rahab that renders it probable that she was a woman of bad reputation. She entertained the Hebrew spies, and afterwards became the wife of the Hebrew prince Salmon.

Matt. i. 5. She was an innkeeper. If the term *zonah*, then, was ever applied to her in a bad sense, it must have belonged to a previous period of her life, for there is no evidence, nor any probability that she was an abandoned woman at the time the Hebrew spies entered Jericho. Naturally, as strangers, and on a mission of so much peril and importance, they would seek a house of private entertainment, such as Rahab kept. The Chaldee calls the woman that Samson lodged with an innkeeper. Schleusner says the word may mean one that prepares and sells food, and receives strangers to entertain them. It must be remembered, however, that in those times female innkeepers trafficked with their personal charms at the same time that they entertained travellers. In view of all the authorities within my reach, I conclude our translators are correct; and consequently this woman was not Samson's wife, and his conduct at Gaza is a most painful specimen of imperfect morality, and full of warning. Truly there is no man so deep but he has some shallow place.

The previous chapter is full of adventure, but the vicissitudes of our hero are by no means ended, though it is twenty years since his victory with the jaw-bone, and his deliverance from dying of thirst at Lehi; still we find trouble following trouble, and no wisdom gleaned from the past. His last years do not bear scrutiny as well as his earlier ones. Considering his mission, and his relation to the Philistines, it is difficult to understand his motives for going into one of their principal cities. It can hardly be supposed that his meeting with the Gazite woman was anything more than accidental. To see her could not have been the main purpose for which he went to Gaza. As he must have been well known, it is passing strange that he should have trusted himself in one of their strongholds, and then should have behaved so imprudently. How could one of his stalwart frame—whose name was a raw-head-and-bloody-bones in all the village stories of Philistia—and of Nazarite hair and beard, have expected to escape notice? It was scarcely necessary for any one from Askelon or Timnath to have pointed him out. At all events, it was soon known in Gaza that Samson was come; and, either because they did not know just where to find him, or being afraid to seize him at once, they set sentinels at the gates. They now felt sure that they had caged the lion, and Samson, though not where he should have been, was not insensible to danger. Aroused at midnight, and suspecting what was intended, he proceeds straight to the gates, and carries away the doors and posts upon his shoulders. The guards were either terror smitten, and not able to face him, or were asleep. They made no resistance, and he seems to have had too much contempt for the gate to kick it down, or too much refinement, for he lifts it off by mere force, and lays it on his shoulders, and carries it away to the top of a hill towards Hebron. The doors of Bible lands are not shaped into an arch, nor fitted into the wall or facing as with us. They had not our hinges. The door fell into sockets below, and was fastened in a projecting bracket above. Such were the doors of Egypt and of the Holy Land. The sepulchres of the Nile and of Jerusalem are proof; and a knowledge of this fact explains the anxious inquiry of the devout women coming to our Lord's tomb, "Who shall roll us away the stone?" That is, lift it out of the groove or socket. The great difficulty in opening such doors was their weight. Samson's strength must, therefore, have been prodigious; since, according to the text, he lifted the heavy town gate, bars, brackets, beams, posts, and all, and carried them to the top of a distant hill. The text does not mean that he carried the city gate all the way to Hebron, which was at least twenty miles from Gaza; literally, " to the top of a hill which looketh towards Hebron;" but we cannot now identify it.

These brief historical notes are perhaps sufficient to ex plain the text. Let us, then, pause with two historical periods before us, and review our story from the top of the rock Etam, and from the top of the hill towards Hebron, where Samson put down the gate of Gaza. These two historic points comprehend twenty years of his life, and a review of them is a fearful warning to all fitful professors of religion, and to all backsliders. Here we see a character great and marvellous for supernatural exploits, spoiled, through a spiritual relapse, and by inconsistencies. Remarkable as is the heroic age of Israel's judges, Samson is certainly the most remarkable of them all. And after all we scarcely get a clear view of his inner life. So thick and heavy are the clouds that hang over him, that if an apostle had not given him a place among spiritual heroes, we should have despaired of him altogether. It is true, however, and in this there is hope, that, amid all his fearful backslidings, he never seems to have forgotten his commission against the Philistines. His conscience was kept faithful to this behest by his own passionate hatred of them. But this is only another proof of God's sovereignty, which maketh the wrath of man to praise him, even as the appetite and relish for our food proves his wisdom and benevolence. It was not enough to make food nourish us; God has made it agreeable to us. So he is pleased to make our duty and our interest in the long run lie in the same line. Duty is pleasure.

While Samson dwelt in Etam, I take it there was a revival of grace in his soul. If so, it was a most critical and deeply interesting period in his life. Suppose we climb up to the top of the rock, and from his retreat look back to the home of his innocent youth at Zorah, and inquire how his mother takes all these things. Ah, his mother! is she yet alive? Then how many conflicting fears and hopes must have filled her mind! Mysterious and wholly inexplicable events have marked her son's life. She remembers well the angel's bright appearance, and how he rode up towards heaven on the smoke of their accepted sacrifice, as if it had been a chariot—and how earnestly she had been commanded to demean herself, and to bring up the child as one pre-eminently consecrated to God, and to be a deliverer of the chosen people. She thinks over and over his strange fancy for the woman of Timnath, and how it was not at all agreeable to her and her husband, that he should marry a Philistine, but that they submitted, hoping it was of the Lord. She is now, too, acquainted with the lion adventure, the bees, and the honey. She recollects the wedding ceremonies, feasting, and riddles, the divorce, and the terrible tragedies at Askelon and at Timnath. She wonders how all this is to fulfil his mission. She hopes, as only a parent can hope; a thousand times does she think over the past, and try to read the future; a thousand times does she interrogate herself, saying, Can this be my Nazarite boy? Are these things realities, or visions and dreams? Where are they all to end? When will the mystery be explained? Oh, how I loved that child! What great hopes I entertained of him! If she had not been a mother of faith and principle equal to her comprehension and penetration of judgment, she could not have sustained herself under such trials.

But what of the hero himself? Think you he retired in disgust from the hip and thigh slaughter? Or did he dwell in the top of the rock Etam for safety? Or after the manner of the lion, having torn as many struggling victims as he could, did he leave them mangled and dying, and seek this solitary abode to gloat over his satisfied revenge? Or did he go up to Etam sulky and proud, like Achilles to his tent on the Ægean shore? Or like a wild Bedouin or Camanche, having revenged his wrongs, does he seek his mountain home, to scowl defiance upon his pursuers from his impregnable fortress? There may have been a mingling of some of these feelings in his breast, when he went up to Etam; but I think his purpose was to escape for a time from all worldly excitements. He was weary of the battle. He felt his life to be a mystery. He was astonished both at his successes and his shortcomings. He saw the mighty power of God in his victories, and his goodness in his own deliverance. He wished, therefore, for a sheltered place—for a quiet and safe retreat for prayer and meditation. Impetuous as he was—tumultuous as his life had been—he was not thoughtless. He has not wholly escaped from the influence of his mother's early lessons, and his father's fervent prayers. He still feels that Nazarite vows are upon him, and though painfully conscious of many sad failures in duty, he has still a deep yearning of soul toward God, and an earnest desire to fulfil his mission, so as to secure the divine approbation. There is with him still space for repentance, and for renewing of his vows. In his retirement, conscious of his many failures, restless thoughts, "like a deadly swarm of hornets armed," must have often rushed upon him. Piety, patriotism, and personal feelings were all working together in him to fulfil his mission. For we must not suppose that God's Spirit is easily discouraged, and departs wholly from a man when he falls once, or even several times, into sin. There is, indeed, a sin unto death, a sin for which no prayer or sacrifice can avail, for which there is no forgiveness. There is a point of rebellion beyond which no pardon can be extended. God's Spirit does sometimes cease to strive with men. Ephraim may be left to his idols, because he would not leave them. Men may quench and grieve away the Spirit of God by which they might be sealed to the day of redemption. But the general rule is, that God's long-suffering is as apparent as his sovereignty. He bears long with the children of men. The Holy Spirit does not abandon the sinner for a slight offence; and sometimes we see a spiritual resurrection after many long years of apparent death. The good seed sown lies long under the cold snows that have fallen from the mountains, but it has not perished. Wordly entanglements and passions have bound it up like the pitched mummy cloths of Egypt; but the seed still has the living germ within it; and at last it springs up in the soul, and blooms into eternal life, it may be, long after the careful parent that sowed it in faith, and watered it with many tears, has entered into rest. Sometimes, also, we see the piety of youth reviving, and again budding, after it has seemed to have suffered a grievous blight, and even to have been uprooted for ever.

Dear parent, after all the frustration of your hopes—after repeated disappointments, hope on—never despair—the root to this very hour that you have planted and watered, though it be long in sprouting, may continue alive; and yet, "through the scent of water it may bud."

We shall do well, also, to remember that it is not without affliction that youthful piety is generally recovered after a relapse. The forcing heat of a furnace may be required, after years of decline, to make the tree "sprout again and send forth its boughs as a plant." It is not the mere scent of water, nor the ordinary shower, nor the ordinary gleams of sunshine, that can revive the plant and make it live in freshness. It is often only the furnace of affliction that can bring us back from backslidings.

I apprehend Samson's experience of grace was not miraculous. Believers in all ages are liable to temptations and relapses. None of them are saints upon earth. The representative or official character of the judges, prophets, and apostles is not to be confounded with their personal piety; and consequently, their experience as believers is to be considered as a fair ensample for us—their experience of the grace of God—their penitence and faith—their hopes and trials—are to be considered as if they were merely believers, and apart from their official characters. David and Paul, as individuals, believed and repented, and were subject to like conflicts with ourselves. The same is true of Moses and Samson. When Moses killed the Egyptian, he fled to the wilderness. An undefined future lay before him. He followed his natural feelings, but was most graciously guided. There, in "meditative solitudes," he communed with God, and pondered over the condition of his countrymen, until the hour came for him to be commissioned to deliver them. And Samson in like manner, not finding his countrymen sympathizing with him—finding that they did not rally around him, and say, Lead us against the Philistines; the Lord is with you; he has raised you up to be a judge in Israel, and an avenger of his people—finding that they were so degraded that they would not second his efforts for their deliverance, and somewhat, no doubt, with the same kind of feelings that Moses had, when he broke the tables of the law—he betook himself to retirement in the rock Etam.

I therefore conclude that "then," in the beginning of the sixteenth chapter, does not mean that he went to Gaza, and made himself vile immediately after the great deliverance God had wrought for him at Lehi. Surely a considerable time must have elapsed after such an experience of God's goodness, before he could have fallen into such a quagmire. "Then" here seems to indicate that at or near to the end of his administration of twenty years, he went to Gaza, and soon after to Sorek. His exploit at Lehi awed the Philistines so that for some twenty years they were comparatively quiet. The time that intervened between Samson at Lehi and Samson fallen at Gaza, adds to his guilt, for he must now have been about forty years of age, and of a varied experience, and should have been more on his guard than to have fallen into the toils of the Gazite woman. In his fall, we see that besetting sins are deceitful and die hardly. They have many lives. When we are ready to suppose them dead, a slight occurrence may awaken them to a vigorous life. In our narrative there is an ominous silence as to how Samson was employed for almost twenty years. All this time he did nothing. It is no wonder then that his inner man has fallen into consumption. And as is always the case, in the proportion that his spiritual life grew weaker and weaker, his sensual grew stronger and stronger, until his constitutionally besetting lust broke forth again, as a fire that has only been smouldering, when it was supposed to have been extinguished. There is no truce in the war between the flesh and the spirit. The one or the other is prevailing. If the house of David waxes stronger, then the house of Saul grows weaker. And the reverse is just as true. Samson's inner life is no doubt the exact type of thousands now. Many suppose when they have experienced some special deliverances as Samson did at Lehi, and have had some evidence of the grace of God, that their besetting sins are overcome; when in fact, they have only retired, and are waiting in ambush just beyond gun shot, till an opportunity is presented for them to return and take the fort by storm, as Samson's did with him at Gaza. It were well to learn, from Samson's sad experience, to be on our guard against besetting sins, especially of the grosser kind. And there is the more need for watchfulness against the lusts of the flesh, because they are favoured in their approaches to the citadel of the heart and conscience by many less constitutional sins, or sins less suspected of being so flagrant and vile, which, however, when indulged prepare the way for their return, and for their violent onset. In the presence of professed friends, the excitement of good feeling, your own self-confidence, a sense of security, and obscuration of divine holiness, a faint view of God's law, and the strong pleadings of nature within—then is the moment when constitutional sinful propensities arouse themselves with a fearfully increased fierceness. And it is just in this manner, and by such slow approaches, and by such carefully prepared intrenchments, the heart is taken. Let all who fancy themselves secure, remember the dreadful warning of Peter—that "if, after, having escaped the pollutions of the world, through the knowledge of the Lord and Saviour Jesus Christ, they are again entangled therein and overcome, the latter end is worse with them than the beginning."

The triumphing of Samson's baser passions at Gazà and Sorek were most certainly preceded by a decaying, consumptive state of his religious character. His piety had almost withered away before he went to Gaza. And it is always thus. One sin leads the way to another. A decay of spiritual life allows greater liberty to the lusts of the flesh. Indolence, gluttony, worldliness, drunkenness, and the pampering of any of the lusts of the flesh are all of kin. They are links in the same hellward dragging chain. The entanglement is not perfected all at once. Absence from the prayer meeting follows the neglect of closet prayer. And a growing neglect of divine worship is followed by a want of relish for God's word, and by a listlessness or want of interest in religious matters, and by a greater degree of pleasure in worldly things; and now the way is fully prepared for carnal nature to rise in rebellion, and with a fiercer frenzy, because of its long apparent quiescence or imprisonment, seize on the spoils. The course of the backslider is fearfully rapid and agonizing in the end. Please read Eph. vi. 10—18; and Col. iii. 1—15. *"Let him that thinketh he standeth take heed lest he fall."*

## CHAPTER XIV.

### THE FATAL SLEEP IN DELILAH'S LAP.

"At-length to lay my head and hallow'd pledge
Of all my strength in the lascivious lap
Of a deceitful concubine, who shore me
Like a tame wether, all my precious fleeces,
Then turn'd me out, ridiculous, despoil'd,
Shaven, and disarm'd among mine enemies."
*Samson's Confession.*

FROM the fourth and following verses of the sixteenth chapter, we have Samson's next adventure. It is with a celebrated beauty of great historic interest, belonging to the vale of Sorek, which probably took its name from the brook that ran through it and fell into the sea near Askelon. This vale was rich and populous, and probably occupied by the best class of the Philistines. The myrtle, the vine, acacia, oleander, olive, pomegranate, and orange were familiar to the eyes of the beautiful Delilah. Milton ignores the woman of Gaza altogether, nor is there any reason to believe she was Samson's wife. But in all his love affairs there is a singular disregard for the daughters of his own people.* And this may be one reason why his "course of

* "La foiblesse du coeur de Samson, dans toute cette histoire, est encore plus étonnante que la force de son corps."—"The weakness of Samson's heart, in all this history, is still more surprising than the strength of his body."—*Calmet.*

love" never ran smoothly. "He always matched improperly, and he was cursed in all his matches." His conduct now, however, is the more mysterious, because he is no longer the young lover, "sighing like a furnace;" but of mature years and experience—the same man who went down to Timnath some twenty years ago, as strong in muscle, but weaker in character. And though his enemies could not find out what constituted his great strength, they were not slow in discovering where his weakness lay; and as ordinary measures had not enabled them to get the secret of his strength, they resolved to overreach him through his fondness for a woman of their own nation.

Of Delilah's father and mother, education and previous character, we know nothing. And I believe she is never mentioned in the Scriptures after her connection with Samson. We do not know what became of her. The name Delilah is believed to signify "humiliation—bringing down to shame—that which humbles and debases." We are not able, however, to explain how her parents happened to give her at birth a name so truly significant and prophetic of the events of her life, that give her a place in the world's history. Were they under a prophetic impulse in giving a name to their child? We are only sure of the historic fact. The names of the Bible are all, probably, descriptive or significant, as oriental names are still, and as all names were originally. Some have doubted whether Delilah was of Philistine parentage. Hebrew tradition and Josephus, however, assert that she was, and this I think the text implies. Some doubt, also, whether she was ever Samson's wife, or only his concubine. Milton considers her his second married wife, which seems to me most likely. It is true, however, she is nowhere called his wife; and if she were his wife, it may be pertinently asked, why did he not take her home to his own house? Though his married wife, as I think, she was chosen from wrong motives or upon corrupt principles. His choice was made in violent passion, rather than from prudence or out of regard to the religion of his fathers. As a Philistine, she belonged to a wicked and idolatrous people.

"The lords of the Philistines" were the chiefs of their five principalities: Gaza, Gath, Askelon, Ashdod, and Ekron. And though these principalities were considered in most respects sovereign and independent, yet in their wars against the Israelites they were generally, perhaps always, united. At this time they were confederate against the Hebrew champion, and diligently watching for an opportunity to get an advantage over him. As soon, therefore, as they heard that Samson had formed an alliance with Delilah, they offered her a large bribe if she would get from him the secret of his strength. Each chief promised to give her eleven hundred pieces of silver, if she succeeded. Five thousand five hundred pieces of silver was a considerable sum of money in those days. If these pieces, as it is probable, were shekels of silver, the sum was about three thousand dollars.

The heathen are all superstitious. Even the Greeks and Romans, with all their enlightenment in philosophy and in the arts and sciences, were the slaves of terrible superstitions. The people of the East generally are given to charms, incantations, signs, and omens. As Samson did not owe his extraordinary strength to the size of his body, the Philistine lords seem to have conjectured that it must lie in some amulet or charm, and that the supernatural power he wielded depended on his continued possession of some magical ring or word; and that if they could in any way get this secret from him, then they could easily make him their prisoner and put him to death.

"And Delilah said unto Samson, Tell me, I pray thee

wherein thy great strength lieth, and wherewith thou mightest be bound to afflict thee? And Samson said unto her, If they bind me with seven green withs, that were never dried, then shall I be weak, and be as another man."

I have nothing to say in defence of Samson's lying. It seems to me, after all that commentators have said in explaining the text so as to excuse at least in part his trifling with Delilah, that she was correct in saying to him that he told her lies. Yes, *lies* is the word, neither white, nor little, nor over-the-shoulder; but in honest English lies. Nor need I explain how his soul was vexed unto death, for he is neither the first nor the last man whose soul has been vexed to death by an ungodly woman. Let us then at once attend to the enticement, the repeated temptation, the struggling of the strong man in the toils of an artful woman, and the success of the beguilement.

The Philistine lords did not profess to wish to kill Samson, but only "to bind him to afflict him;" that is, according to the Hebrew, "to humble him, to bring him low." "Entice him," said they, "and see wherein his great strength lieth;" literally, "for what cause his strength is so great." Much as Delilah may have been to blame, I should think she did not intend to do all she did. She did not expect consequences to be what they really were. She did not see the ultimate purpose of her seducers. Nor did she know that Samson would in fact be so powerless, and that they would tear out his eyes—those very eyes that gazed upon her in such rapturous love—and load him with chains, and carry him off to grind in the mills of Gaza.

The best excuse I can make for Delilah is, that out of curiosity—the very same thing that is thought to have wrought such mischief with our first mother—she desired to experiment with her husband, and find out the secret of his extraordinary strength, but expecting every time that he would be able to extricate himself from all difficulty—not believing it possible that his enemies could finally and fatally prevail against him.

"If they bind me," said Samson, "with seven green withs that were newly dried." Withs, according to the Hebrew here, may have been any kind of tough, pliable wood, twisted into ropes. The Septuagint says they were cords made of rawhide, and so the Vulgate, *nerviceis funibus*. It is probable the first cords or ropes used were thongs cut from rawhide, twisted and dried. Tugs are extensively used even in our day, instead of iron chains, for drawing the plow, cart, harrow, and wagon in Africa, and many other parts of the world. I have seen ropes made of the fibres of the bog-wood, in Ireland, and of young hickories, hazels, or osiers, in our Southern and Western States. In India, wild buffaloes and elephants when first caught are bound with green withs. When green they are exceedingly strong, but when dried they are brittle and good for nothing. New ropes, withs, and the sacred number, seven, seem all to have been suggested by his knowledge of their superstitious ideas of a charm or spell, for such things were used in heathen incantations. The monuments show that flax was used long before this time in Egypt, and ropes of hemp may also have been in use; but those made of fibres of trees, or of switches, were not and are not still superseded.

"Now there were men lying in wait, abiding with her in the chamber," or rather hidden in the inner apartment, not present in the same room, who rushed out upon him; "but Samson broke the withs as a thread of tow is broken when it toucheth the fire. So his strength was not known." The experiment with the new ropes resulted as the one with the new withs had done. But still Delilah persists, and he tells her to weave the seven locks of his head with the web.

Biblical scholars tell us this thirteenth verse ends abruptly, that it should be as the Septuagint has it, closing with directions how to fasten his hair, just as she accordingly does, as we are told in the next verse. This is certainly the sense. "The seven locks" probably means the seven divisions into which his hair was platted. As a Nazarite he was obliged to wear his hair long, and as a matter of comfort, it was necessary to weave it into locks, or distinct folds, and the number seven being sacred, it was adopted. It was equivalent to all his hair. "And she fastened it," that is, his hair in its seven-fold form, to the loom, winding it about the yard-beam, as is plain from the verses following.

This third experiment was a much more dangerous one than the preceding; it approached so near to his awful secret that we begin to tremble for him. He is now beginning to handle sharp-edged tools. The circle is growing smaller and smaller with fearful rapidity. He tells his enchantress, if his long locks were woven around the beam of the loom, he would be as another man. And she to make the experiment more sure, fastened the web to the floor or wall with a pin. But as he was still possessed of the mark of his covenant with Jehovah, so the Philistines could not prevail against him. He dragged the whole loom, web, pin, beam, and all by his hair.

But does Samson now arouse himself, and say, I have trifled long enough; away, fair tempter, I cannot stay any longer on this dangerous ground; I cannot sin against God, and do so wicked a thing as to betray my secret? Alas! the woman's importunities prevail. "He told her all that was in his heart." So great was his infatuation that, like the moth, he approached nearer and nearer to the flame, until he was consumed by it. He told her of his wondrous birth, and eventful life, and divine deliverances; that he was a Nazarite, and that the preservation of his long hair was a test of his obedience, and a token of the divine presence to aid him whenever opportunity presented for executing justice upon her countrymen; and that if his hair were shaven he would be as another man, because by such a sin he would deprive himself of the divine power that was vouchsafed to him as long as he was faithful to his vows. She saw, by his earnest tone, and subdued and sincere manner, that he was no longer amusing her, but had actually told her the secret of his strength. But instead of being favourably impressed by this mark of his confidence, or moved from her satanic purpose of pressing her experiments by this proof of his honesty, and of his ardent love for her, she immediately took measures to betray him. Accordingly she makes such positive assurances to the Philistine lords that they are not to be trifled with this time, that they hurry up to Sorek with the money in hand. And she tells them that he has told her at last the secret of his heart, and they counted out the money. And sure enough, this time her plan succeeds, as I would fain hope even beyond her own wishes.

"And she made him sleep upon her knees." At noon, in the East, it is very hot, and the inhabitants are in the habit of taking a *siesta*. This short repose is usually taken by a son in the lap of his mother, or by a husband in the lap of his wife. The climate and fixtures of their domestic establishments are suited for such a luxury. The woman sits on a divan, or mat, or carpet, crosslegged, and the man lays himself down with his head in her lap, "and she gently taps, strokes, sings, and soothes him to sleep."

"And she called for a man, and caused him to shave off the seven locks of his head." Most, if not all, the pictures I have ever seen of Samson in Delilah's lap, represent her with a pair of scissors, cutting off his hair with her own hands. This is altogether wrong. It may well be doubted whether scissors were then in use. It is, however, well known that barbers by profession are nearly as old as the creation. They are found on the oldest monuments of the Nile; and the monuments of the Tigris and Euphrates, as well as of Egypt, prove that wig wearing was very common in a very remote antiquity. The Arabian Nights and Oriental tales speak of barbers as belonging to an ancient and important profession. The embalming surgeon of Egypt seems to have been also a common barber.

While Samson sleeps, the barber takes off his sacred locks. So skilful were the barbers of the East that they are said to have been able to take off a man's beard or hair without awaking him, nay, rather to have lulled him to sweeter sleep by the operation.

I do not understand Samson to say, in the seventeehth verse, that his great strength existed essentially in his hair. All Nazarites had long hair, but they did not all possess superhuman strength, nor strength in proportion as their hair was long. Samson is not, therefore, to be understood as saying that his hair was essentially his strength, or that his strength was natural, but that his hair was the mark of his Nazarite relation to God, whose Spirit imparted to him his miraculous strength. He meant that his long hair was a proof of his obedience, and of his covenant with God, from whom he derived and would always derive strength so long as he was obedient to him. And consequently, if he were disobedient, and his hair were shaven, then the Nazarite vow that consecrated him to God would be broken, and God would abandon him, and he would become weak as another man. The secret was now out, and the plot was speedily executed. "And she began to afflict him, and his strength went from him." This she did herself, before she called for the Philistines, to see whether he were really weak now as another man. And though she is now convinced that he has lost his strength, she still probably thought it was only for a little time, and that in actual extremity he would recover it again.

How deep must have been Samson's mortification! How terrible his agony and disappointment, to find that he had broken his vows, and was indeed forsaken of God! At first he was not conscious of his awful fall: "He awoke out of his sleep, and said, I will go out as at other times before, and shake myself. And he wist not that the Lord was departed from him. But the Philistines took him and put out his eyes, and brought him down to Gaza, and bound him with fetters of brass; and he did grind in the prison house." His sleeping was accursed, and more accursed his waking. "He that sleeps in sin must look to wake in loss and weakness."* There may be those who think that Samson could not have been so easily overcome. It is wonderful that, after he had been three times tried, and had found each time that the Philistines were lying in wait, within call, to come upon him, he allowed Delilah to dally with him a fourth time, and then told her the real secret of all his strength. His infatuation was most extraordinary; but inordinate and unlawful attachments of this kind have generally been found to be at the bottom of the most horrid and revolting deeds in the chronicles of strong men. Remember David, and beware of the weakness of human nature.

But it is not to be supposed that we have here a full account of all the interviews or conversations that passed between Samson and Delilah. He was a judge in Israel, and however ardent his passions may have been, it is not at all likely that he surrendered without a struggle. We know

* Bishop Hall.

that she had to apply all her arts repeatedly. She watched for moments most favourable to her designs. She found out by what arts of soft dalliance she could obtain the greatest influence over him. She resorted to every means of lulling his suspicions. He seems not to have known of the bribe, nor at first of her intercourse with his national enemies. And even after he found that she had the Philistines lying in wait to rush upon him, as soon as she fancied he had told her his secret, he was easily persuaded that it was all in jest. Perhaps she flattered him, and told him she loved to see him displaying his great strength, and making sport of the Philistines. Nor did he fall in a moment, nor in an hour. Doubtless several days, it may be weeks or months, intervened; time enough for his resentment to cool, or for removing his suspicions, and for her to ply all her arts of persuasion and blandishment. Once and again he visits Sorek, and every time she gains some new point of influence over him. She conducts the siege with admirable skill. Simple minded and confiding as he was strong, he is at last surprised and taken. We have no record of his internal conflict, but the battle in his great soul must have been a terrific struggle before he yielded. There seems to have been less prudence, and not so much firmness as he displayed with his first wife. He gave his Timnite bride at first a flat refusal when she attempted to get his secret. But he had not courage to give a direct and emphatic *No* to Delilah at all. She plied her arts, and succeeded in lulling his suspicions, until he told her all his heart, and said, "I have been a Nazarite unto God from my mother's womb."

How are the mighty fallen! What a confession to be made in the lap of Delilah! What a sad commentary upon his education and youthful hopes! Why did not the very utterance of such words arouse him to a sense of his shame? Why did he not flee as for his life? Strange that he was so infatuated that he did not even now, at this late hour, break away at all hazards from the enchantress! But it is just so now. He that departs from God hardens his heart and sears his conscience, and soon falls into the fatal habit of disregarding the warnings of his conscience and of God's word. To dally with Delilah is fatal. The only safety is flight.

## CHAPTER XV.

### A GRIST FROM THE PRISON MILL OF GAZA.

"In that tale I find
The furrows of long thought, and dried-up tears,
Which ebbing, leave a sterile track behind,
O'er which all heavily the journeying years
Plod the last sands of life—where not a flower appears."
*Childe Harold.*

WHEN Josephus says Samson was a prophet, he means that he was raised up by a particular providence, and set apart to God's service as a Nazarite, and had an extraordinary commission from God for avenging his people: and not that he had any prophetic revelations. Such revelations were not made by him; nevertheless he was a great teacher. In him we see the workings of human nature, and the deep strugglings of higher principles, both in prosperity and adversity. But he has fallen—sadly fallen through the fascinations of an ungodly, unprincipled woman. The tempest that had so often before nearly made shipwreck of our giant judge, has at last stranded him on the beach. And scarcely was Christendom more convulsed at the fall of Sebastopol, than was all Philistia at the capture of Samson.

"The Philistines took him, and put out his eyes, and brought him down to Gaza, and bound him with fetters of brass; and he did grind in the prison-house."

Delilah's fourth experiment succeeded, perhaps, even beyond her expectations; and when the Lord departed from Samson, instead of being able to carry away the doors of Gaza on his shoulders, he is now led thither a helpless captive—blind and in chains. How sad the change! But more humiliating far the cause of this change, than the ignominy of his external sufferings. Now the very arms that once wielded the new jaw-bone with such terrible effect, and rent asunder the new cords and withs as burnt tow, are bound hard and fast in fetters of brass. An insulting guard of uncircumcised Dagon-worshippers taunt and goad him along the weary road down to Gaza: Aha! this is the way you carry off our doors from the city gate, is it? Don't you wish you could find another jaw-bone? Cowardly wretches; but yesterday ten thousand of you could not stand before him, nor could you now, had he only been faithful to his God! But such is always the way of transgression—such are always the consequences of departing from the living God. Those sacred locks that had been tenderly cherished by his mother, and hitherto so much cared for by himself, are left in Sorek, the spoils and the sport of a faithless woman and her accomplices in crime. His gait and bearing are not now as of yore. That head, so long adorned with glossy locks, sealing his birth-consecration to Jehovah, is now bald and exposed to a Syrian sun. His steps, once so steady and so firm, are now feeble and tripping. The eyes, that once gazed upon the heavens in rapt devotion, and were wont to speak flames of love, or shoot forth the fire of anger, are now rayless, never again to kindle with the light of the sun. Newly blind, he hobbles along, not having yet learned how to walk without his eyes. How different his return, from his defiant departure from the same city with its doors upon his shoulders!

"And the Philistines put out his eyes." We are told

that in Persia, it is the practice of the king to punish a rebellious city by exacting so many pounds of eyes, and that in fulfilling this order, his executioners go and "scoop out from every one they meet, till they have the weight required." Learned authors agree in saying that the common way of putting out the eyes among the Greeks and Asiatics, was "by drawing or holding a red-hot iron before them." This awful custom is still known in Asia and Africa. Sometimes, but not usually, the eyes were cut out, and sometimes dug out with a dagger and carried to the king in a basin, after the manner of John the Baptist's head to Herodias' daughter. The evidence is full that such acts of cruelty were common in ancient times. And sometimes, history informs us, the executioners ordered to destroy the eyes of prisoners were so careless that the prisoners lost their lives under the operation. M. Bonomi, in his "Nineveh and its Palaces," (p. 169,) furnishes us with a drawing from Khorsabad, that illustrates this savage barbarity. The engraving is copied from the sculpture on the chamber of the palace of the king. The central figure is the king himself, and before him are three prisoners, the foremost one on his knees in a most beseeching attitude, and the other two standing behind in humble posture, begging for mercy. The king is thrusting the point of his spear into one of the eyes of the suppliant before him, while with his left hand he holds the ends of cords fastened to the upper lips of the other captives, who are manacled and fettered, and standing behind the one whose eyes are about to be put out. The king is attended also by his cup-bearer and officers of state, bearing sceptres; by a eunuch and the chief governor, or *Rab Signeen*. Who knows but that this is the history of king Zedekiah from 2 Kings illustrated?

"And bound him with fetters of brass." The Philistines were so terribly afraid of Samson, that they not only put out his eyes, but bound him. Though his arms were now as feeble as any other man's, yet his bodily presence was to them as king Edward's skin and armour were to the border clans. They were determined that if by any means his strength should return to him, so that he should break the fetters with which he was bound, yet he should not have eyes to see how to use it. The "brass" of the text is *copper*, for as yet the factitious metal known to us as brass was not in use. We have ample proof, however, of the use of copper in remote ages for many purposes to which iron is now applied. Ancient monuments show conclusively that chains, fetters, instruments for labour and for cooking, knives, axes, and vases, dishes, and dice boxes, hammers, chisels, adzes, and hatchets, daggers, rings, prisoners' fetters, and strong chains were all used by the ancients. Such articles, and a bowl of bitumen overlaid with copper and a piece of lead, have been brought from the ruins of the Tigris and Euphrates, and are now in the British Museum. Those brought from Tel Sifx in ancient Babylon by Mr. Loftus,* seem to have been the stock in trade of a coppersmith, whose forge was near by. Copper was used in ancient Egypt, where the art of hardening the points of their copper instruments seems to have been more perfectly known than it is in the present day. The obelisks of the Nile are covered with hieroglyphics, and yet they are so hard, that it is with great difficulty any inscriptions can be cut on them with our tools. The cutting of the French inscriptions on the obelisk set up by Louis Philippe in the *Place de la Concorde*, is in proof of this. We find the Israelites using copper abundantly in building the tabernacle. Though iron was not wholly unknown to the ancients, it was not much used. It will be readily remembered, however, that the

* Loftus's Travels and Researches in Babylonia and Susiana, p. 269. See also Layard's Nineveh—*passim*.

Bible speaks in several places of chains and fetters of brass (copper.) See, particularly, Psalms xlix. 8; 2 Kings xxv. 7, and the history of Manasseh and Hezekiah. Mr. Layard thinks the fetters of the prisoners at Nineveh were of *iron*, but it is generally conceded that the monuments prove that those of Egyptian prisoners were of copper. Mr. Loftus thinks that the Chaldeans were a colony from Egypt. The best authorities, as we have seen, agree that the Philistines were of Egyptian origin. It were a deeply interesting subject, but one that does not come within my present purpose, to trace out from ancient history and the readings of recent discoveries, the striking similarities that exist between the ancient Egyptians, Assyrians, and Philistines. Modern researches and discoveries all tend to corroborate the unity of the human races, and their dispersion from a common cradle, according to the tenth and eleventh chapters of Genesis.

I think this is the first time the Bible speaks of putting out any one's eyes; and the first time that we have mention made of a prison since the record of Pharaoh's round house, in the history of Joseph. The sculptured records of the East prove, however, the great antiquity of the usages referred to in the text. The ancients were in the habit of keeping some of their prisoners to grace a great feast or triumphal procession, and in the mean time of heaping upon them every possible insult and cruelty that life could bear.

It is well known that the Indians of America delight in such cruelties. They inflict wounds on their prisoners, and treat them in the most cruel manner, that they may see how much courage they have, and enjoy their writhings of pain. Sometimes the prisoners are made to run the gauntlet, or to dance and sing through the most exquisite sufferings from wounds or from the slowly consuming flames, until death releases them.

In the mean time Samson is not only bound, but made to grind at the mills as a slave, and as a slave of the state. His condition was in every respect a most painfully aggravated one—much more so than if he had been reduced to servitude in a private family, whose self-interest, if no higher motives were found, would prompt them to mild treatment. Here is the original of imprisonment at hard labour. I presume this is the first instance of penitentiary labour on record, and I think it is the only instance in the Bible of imprisonment and hard labour united. The oriental custom with prisoners was either a summary execution, when not reserved for a triumph, or condemnation to perpetual servitude. From Lam. v. 11, and Isa. xlvii. 2, it appears that the Chaldeans made such of their Hebrew captives as they wished especially to degrade, to grind in the mill. Herodotus says that the Scythians put out the eyes of all their prisoners of war, and made them milkers of their cows. Probably they considered blind slaves better for milking, and for grinding, somewhat as we put a blind horse, or a blind-folded one to turn the wheel in sawing wood, and for the performance of like rotary work.

In Zanzibar and Eastern Africa, as well as in portions of Asia and on many of the islands of the sea, this kind of primitive mill and the mortar are the only instruments in use for grinding. The Cassada root, ground or pounded, is the staple food of the poorer classes. The mill consists of two flat circular stones, some two feet in diameter. "The one is convex, having a hole through which the grain passes, and is supported upon the other, which is concave, by a firm peg. To the upper stone is affixed a handle, by which it is kept revolving by two women sitting on opposite sides of the mill." (Osgood's Notes, p. 26.)

So necessary was the mill considered in a family, that according to the law of Moses, "no man shall take the nether or the upper millstone to pledge, for he taketh a man's life to pledge." That is, his life and that of his family depended on his having a mill by which to prepare their bread. The same law substantially prevails among us. The constable cannot take by a suit at law the miner's tools, the farmer's plough, nor the mechanic's saw and chisel.

The prophet expressed the utter desolation of Babylon by saying: "The sound of the millstone shall be heard no more at all." That is, it shall become a mass of ruins. The means of subsistence shall wholly cease. This prophecy has been literally fulfilled. All that is now to be seen in the marshes and by "the standing pools" of Babylon, are ruins, a solitary traveller and a few flitting, robbing Bedouins.

Mills are probably as old as looms, and both go back to remotest times. Hand-mills resembling those of the most ancient monuments are still in use in China, Africa, and the East generally. Grain was first prepared for bread probably by boiling it and then bruising it in a mortar. The mortar and pestle are still in use among the aborigines of this continent for pounding or grinding acorns and grain into meal. And the opinion prevails among not a few, that meal obtained in this way is sweeter than that ground in our common mills. The Anglo-Saxons of an early period used the same kind of mills that are found in the East, and this may be another proof of what Dr. Pritchard affirms in a recent work, the Asiatic origin of the Celts. The first mills were probably turned by women, slaves, and prisoners, and in process of time by oxen and donkeys, and then by wind and water, and now by steam. Several allusions are made in the Bible to women grinding at the mill, which are explained in the custom just described. The Philistines designed, by making Samson grind at the mill, to show their vindictive contempt for him. In making him grind with women and slaves for their sport, they also made him work for us. For his eventful history helps us to understand somewhat more fully the awful verities of God, and the sublime teachings of a world to come. Blind and grinding at the mill—a close prisoner and in terrible suffering, he is entitled to our deepest sympathies. His condition is a deeply impressive illustration that the Scriptures of God speak truth in warning us that if we sow to the flesh, we shall of the flesh reap corruption—a harvest of sorrow. Every step of Samson's life warns us of snares in which our own feet may be taken. Along the line of his dark passage from a religious education and early piety, till we find him

"Eyeless in Gaza, at the mill with slaves!"

a prisoner in the temple of the heathen fish-god, there are many points where we should ruminate; and as we look through the window upon his gloomy cell, and hear the shouts of derision in the streets, our gratitude should be excited for the preventing grace of God that has made us to differ. In following him, there are many sharp turns and dark windings and slippery places, where we have great need of the light of the sanctuary to keep our own feet from falling.

I. In Samson's history we see the wonderful forbearance of God, notwithstanding his misuse of great mercies and of supernatural strength. Though he has often fallen, and his life thus far sadly disappoints us, still he was not powerless till he gave up the secret of his strength. Strange, that at his time of life, when the fires of youth should at least have so far cooled down as to be under the control of reason, he should go from Gaza to Sorek. But he was not an exception to the rule, that "because sentence against an evil work is not executed speedily, therefore the heart of the sons of men is fully set in them to do evil." With Samson, as with men now, success made him confident and careless in sinning. Continued prosperity in evil-doing is frequently assumed to be a tenure in perpetuity of the blessings which are thus abused; whereas such abuses enhance every moment the guilt that will be all the more terrible in its results because the judgment has been delayed. Samson's consecration to God before his birth; his birth twice heralded by an angel; his early and most careful religious training; the prayers, sacrifices, and pious hopes of his godly parents; and God's grace given to him in his youth, and all the miraculous strength he had received—all his experience of divine power and goodness through an extraordinary life, only enhanced his guilt, and gave poignancy to his grief as we see him at Gaza. The light of nature accuses all men of sin, so that they are without excuse; but Samson's sins were the more aggravated because they were committed after repeated warnings and singular deliverances. He sinned against the seventh commandment, and under the historic light of signal vengeance upon the nations of old for their uncleanness. He could not have been ignorant that it was for licentiousness the world was destroyed by a flood, and the Canaanites accursed, and twenty-three thousand of the children of his own people had been slain, leaving their bones to bleach on the sand on their way up from Egypt. But if we see the wonderful forbearance of God in Samson's history—what shall we say of the divine patience in our own? Except the power to perform miracles, we have as much as he had to enhance our responsibilities. The greater the degree of gospel light that shines on us, the more is our obligation increased, and our guilt augmented, if we are disobedient. Instead of Nazaritish vows, we are under solemn baptismal obligations, which extend over our whole term of life. Samson's long hair was the sign or test of his obedience. So is our baptism. Dear reader, are you sure you are not guilty of wiping away the sacred drops by which you were publicly dedicated to God, as Samson was shorn of his locks by disclosing the secret of his strength? Have you not at the age of maturity refused to confirm the confession of faith and vows made in your behalf, at your baptism, by your parents? And are none of you still wearing the outward badge of your covenant with God, who are living in known sin? Do you not remember that as baptized persons you are under solemn pledges "to crucify the flesh with its affections and lusts, and to live soberly, righteously, and godly in this present evil world?"

II. Samson lost his great strength in an unconscious manner. His frame was not convulsed when the barber removed his locks. No sobs revealed the fact that he had become as another man. He slept on just as other men sleep, but when he awoke, he is as other men, saving that he is now more degraded. When the Philistines come upon him, he finds himself really as weak as other men, and is soon overpowered.

> "Even as a dove, whose wings are clipped for flying
> Flutters her idle stumps, and still relying
> Upon her wonted refuge, strives in vain
> To quit her life from danger, and attain
> The freedom of her air-dividing plumes;
> She struggles often, and she oft presumes
> To take the sanctuary of the open fields;
> But, finding that her hopes are vain, she yields—
> Even so poor Samson."—*Quarles.*

III. Samson's history is a pictorial of the progressive downward tendencies of sinning. Glorious were the hopes of his infancy. Brightly shone his morning sun in the camp between Eshtaol and Zorah; but soon he is astray at Timnath, and then repentant on the top of Etam, then sinning at Gaza, but delivered by the great mercy of God, but only delivered to go to Sorek, and to fall a victim to Delilah's fascination. And in his case, too, we see that the progress was made through the senses, and that the organ of sense chiefly offending was made the chief sufferer. He went down to Timnath and saw a woman that pleased him His eyes led him astray. But as yet, though smitten, he can hardly be said to have begun his wayward course, for he goes and consults his father and mother about the woman. But time for deliberation and the indulgence of his parents only strengthen his passion for the maiden. From seeing her he talks with her, and his parents talk for him, and at last he is married, but he does not regain paradise by marrying a Philistine. For a good while we know but little of him; doubtless he has found much to regret, but still is far from being established in grace, for by and by we find him very unexpectedly at Gaza, in a most shameful career of guilt; and when delivered by supernatural strength, he is delivered only to go and involve himself more deeply than ever with another Philistine woman. Truly his conduct almost paralyzes our attempts at explanation.

No doubt his overt acts of sinning were preceded, as is always the case with backsliders, by a gradual and secret consumption of his inner life. Our surprise is not so much at his shameless fall in Gaza, as at his backsliding so rapidly as to allow himself to fall at Sorek, so soon again after his miraculous deliverance from the Gazites. But the stupefying and hardening process and deceitfulness of a course of sinning is seen, also, in his gradual approach to ruin in sporting with Delilah. There was a sort of "method in his madness," but all tending to his fall. He tells her to bind him "with seven green withs," as though jestingly he had said, Bind me with a straw, you know I am so fond of you, you can do anything you wish with me. And when he tells her to weave the seven locks of his head, we find him sporting with sacred things. Now it is plain he is lost. His enchantress is within the guards; the sentinels are all past; a little more cunning and perseverance, and she wins. "She has allured him to the brink of the precipice, where his senses reel and sicken, and get to be quite useless, and as good as abandoned him." As he decayed in spiritual life, so the Lord departed from him. But like most miserable backsliders, he was surprised that the Lord had really forsaken him. He fancied he could have proceeded with perfect impunity to such extremities. He was not prepared to find himself forsaken. But his experience soon convinced him that he had not only lost the graces and gifts with which he had been endowed, but as he struggled and fell under the rude grasp of his blood-thirsty enemies, he finds that the Lord had indeed departed from him. And, doubtless, if we could read the inner history of thousands of living men who are fulfilling the lusts of the flesh and of the mind, we should find that their departure from the principles of their pious education had been quite accurately typified in Samson's downward course. There is something alarming and mournful in the fact that the pious resolutions of many men, and the feelings of their early years, will not be awakened till they are on a death-bed, or at the judgment seat of Christ.

We are prone to forget that strength of character in evil or in good is a growth, and may be a slow and imperceptible growth. The oak is called the monarch of the forest, but is not of mushroom growth. First the acorn sprouted, the tiny leaf appeared, the rains bathed it, the winds rocked it, the sun gladdened it; and as it grew its capacities enlarged, and its arms were stretched out for more air, and dew, and sunshine, and its roots went down deeper into the earth, to draw up from thence the necessary sustenance and support. Frosts and snows became as efficient educators as light, and air, and dew; and after many changing seasons of day and night, cold and heat, sunshine and storm, the tree was crowned monarch of the forest. And so it is in the education of our children. Their development is by degrees; their mental and moral powers are a growth as well as their bodies; and all the discipline and educators of the world in which they live are necessary to give them strength and beauty. They must be cared for and protected—they must receive discipline and culture from misfortunes as well as from success. They will have to pass through long dreary days as well as through bright and joyous ones. Books and men, persons and things, the whole living world of art and of nature, are constantly giving them lessons; and more than everything else, the example of their own parents and immediate associates. The fireside is the world's greatest university. The great masses of mankind do not receive the honours of a college, but all are graduates of the hearth. The learning of the books and the lectures of university halls may moulder and rust in the storehouse of memory, but the simple lessons of home, enamelled upon the years of childhood, defy the decay of years. In attempting to clean and restore an old portrait, it sometimes happens that a brighter picture is revealed beneath the old one. So it may be with youth and manhood. The first picture on the canvass is the one drawn in our tenderest years, and though it may be covered over by others, it is imperishable; and as time ripens, and we approach nearer to eternity, it will shine through the outward picture, and perhaps wholly eclipse it. Early impressions are the strongest, and the last to fade from the memory. The home fireside is the greatest institution God has furnished for the education of our race, and his truth is the most powerful agent for enlightening and forming the mind.

We have said before and we repeat it again, it is upon family culture and training, more than anything else, we place our hope for the future of our country. Corruption is the plague of Republics. It makes them weak, and then they fall an easy prey to a military despot. Nor is any system of mere morality and civilization sufficient to stand against the corrupting influences of wealth segregated from christianity. History also proves, beyond cavil, that it is not enough to cry out against corruption when it comes. It is then too late. Demosthenes did this. Cicero did the same; and yet both Athens and Rome perished. Resistance was made too late. The only effectual stand that can be against it is in the nursery. Our homes must be the training places of virtue and religion. The mother and the father must be the great teachers of the household. The father must maintain discipline and morality, and the mother must instil the sweet lessons of pious sentiments, and of stern morality, amidst a corrupting and sensual age. When all our wives are "chaste, keepers at home," and thoroughly awake to their high behests as the mothers of the model Republic; and instead of fluttering in silk for public admiration, make it a paramount duty to teach their sons the principles of honour, patriotism, and integrity, then we shall underwrite with confidence the perpetuity of our liberties.

Then as patriots and friends of the Great Redeemer, we must increase our contributions and personal efforts to advance true religion in the world. We must not sit still in inglorious ease, until the ruins of our distinctive institutions bury us and the hopes of mankind invested in us. We must be up and at the powers of avarice, prejudice, selfishness, ignorance, and irreligion. No time is to be lost. While we sleep the enemy sows tares; and besides, the day is far spent already, and the night cometh when no man can work.

IV. Once more, the downward course of the Hebrew judge illustrates our reluctance to give up the last badge [illegible] We find him [illegible]

ings of the impenitent begin. The giant judge is now a flaming beacon on the brow of ruin. Eyeless and grinding like the vilest slave; but his bodily sufferings and his disgrace are nothing to his mental anguish. The pains of hell get hold of him. Beware, Oh, beware of the lusts of the flesh, which

> "Weave the winding sheet of souls,
> And lay them in the urn of everlasting death."

# CHAPTER XVI.

## THE FINAL CONTEST AND TRAGEDY.

——"All the contest is now
'Twixt God and Dagon.——
This day the Philistines a popular feast
Here celebrate in Gaza; and proclaim
Great pomp, and sacrifice, and praises loud
To Dagon, as their God :—
With sacrifices, triumph, pomp and games,
Of gymnic artists, wrestlers, riders, runners,
Jugglers, and dancers, antics, mummers, mimics.
——Samson is dead.
How died he? Death to life is crown or shame."

*Milton.*

In Judges xvi. 21–30, we have a remarkable tragedy upon a feast—a tragedy, however, not as is often the case at feasts, from the fiends that lurk in the wine cups; but as a judgment of God upon Dagon and his followers, in vindication of his prime minister, and for the deliverance of his people. At the beginning of this great feast the Israelitish judge was in a sad plight. His eyes have been put out, and loaded with brazen fetters he is made to grind at the mill. And yet it were better for him to be thus employed than to have his eyes and lie in Delilah's lap. Better for him to be grinding at the prison mill in Gaza, than to be in Sorek. He was more blind with his eyes in Delilah's lap, than he was without them in the prison—a greater slave when he served her, than when he ground meal for the Philistines. He saw not his sins till he had no eyes. Then he began to receive the true illumination. Then he began to repent and as he repented and was forgiven, his strength began to return to him. "God chasteneth us as sons. He loveth us bleeding;" and when we have smarted enough, we shall feel his loving-kindness. There was a just retribution in putting out his eyes, for they were the instruments of his sinning. It was the lust of the eye that led him astray. But now this organ will lead him no more into temptation.

"Howbeit the hair of his head began to grow again, after it was shaven." It was natural that his hair should grow again, but as the mere hair of his head did not constitute essentially his superior strength, so we must look for his power in the coming conflict to a supernatural source. He lost his strength because by losing his hair he had put himself out of his condition of Nazariteship. He had violated his birth consecration. By disobedience he lost his strength; but by sovereign mercy, the grace of repentance is given to him; and as his hair grows, which was natural, so his strength returns, which is supernatural, and returns in the proportion that he increased in grace, and was restored to the divine favour. Convinced of his great sin in this whole affair—sensible of his weakness and folly—again in his right mind, penitent and earnestly imploring forgiveness, and renewing his vows with a deeper sense of his own unworthiness and dependence upon almighty grace than ever before, he is again at peace with God. But the wretched Philistines knew nothing of all this. They saw not the strugglings of his great soul, and were ignorant of the growth of his inner life. They were incapable of appreciating his anguish of spirit, even if they perceived it. And it is even so now; the life of a true believer is in part hidden from the world. His principles, joys and sorrows, hopes and fears, the men of the world do not understand, neither can they, for they are spiritually discerned. Samson is now chiefly concerned with his own heart. The loss of his eyes, and the labour of turning the mill, and the gibes and coarse laughter of his old enemies were nothing to him, in comparison with his soul's conflict. He heeded not the outer world. His whole soul is now intent on recovering God's favour. And as he grew in true repentance and re-devotement, so his strength began to return to him, and his hair, which was the sign of his covenant with God and of his hold upon omnipotent power, began to grow also. In his recovery, therefore, we have a correspondence between the outward sign and the inward grace. The progressive growth of his hair intimates his progressive repentance towards God, and his growth in the divine favour. As his recovery progressed, his meditations in his gloomy cell and in his toil at the prison mill must have been exceedingly varied, and his feelings intense—now of self-reproach, and then of hope; now of keenest grief, and then of rejoicing in the overpowering sense of divine forgiveness, and in the dawning hope, that yet he should be able to signalize in some remarkable way the termination of his mission as a deliverer of Israel. His experience in his dreary darkness and almost hopeless drudgery, must have been, like his life in general, an extraordinary one. It is not for us to picture out the tumults, despairings, and hopes, and at last rejoicings of his soul. It was doubtless with him as it is with believers now; all his mere reasoning failed, and he was compelled to seek refuge in the precious promises of Him who is able and willing to forgive us our sins, if we confess and forsake them. For the blood of his son Jesus Christ cleanseth us from all sin.

II. But wicked as the Philistines were, they were a religious people, according to the religion of their nation. "Then the lords of the Philistines gathered them together, for to offer a great sacrifice unto Dagon their god, and to rejoice; for they said, Our god hath delivered Samson our enemy into our hand. And when the people saw him, they praised their god; for they said, Our god hath delivered into our hands our enemy and the destroyer of our country, which slew many of us."

After very careful examination of all the authorities within my reach, I am confident there is nothing in the text that is not abundantly sustained by ancient history and recent discoveries. The most probable derivation of the name *Dagon* is from *Dag*, a fish. Some heathen writers seem to have spoken of the same god under the name *Derceto*, and some by the name *Astarte*. At least they have ascribed the same form and attributes to a divinity known by each of these names. According to Lucian* this god was first a fish with a man's head, and then with a woman's head. Diodorus Siculus† says this god had "the head of a woman, and all the rest of the body was like a fish."‡ Milton both in his Paradise Lost and in Samson Agonistes makes Dagon "a sea-idol," part man and part fish. There is a well known passage in Horace's Art of Poetry, which I have not a doubt is an allusion to the idea then prevailing of this sea-

* Lucian De Deâ Syrâ.

† Diodorus Siculus, lib. ii.

‡ The learned Calmet says the same: Desinet in piscem mulier formosa superne." Consult also Selden de Diis Syris, c. 3. de Dagone. The fragments of Berosus referred to may be seen in Cory's Fragments: p. 30, as preserved by Appollodorus. See also Beyr's commentary and Abarbanel's on 1 Samuel; Layard's Nineveh and its Remains, English ed. vol. ii, p 466, 7. Also Layard's Discoveries, second expedition, New York ed. p. 344, etc.

god Dagon. Supposing, says he, a painter join a human head to a horse's neck; or, in Francis's translation:

> "Or if he gave to view a beauteous maid
> Above the waist, with every charm array'd,
> Should a foul fish her lower parts infold,
> Would you not smile such pictures to behold?"

Nor should we forget the fact in proof of this fish-god's worship on the eastern shore of the Mediterranean, that there were at least two cities in Palestine, called Beth-Dagon, that is, the house or temple of Dagon. Joshua xv. 41; xix. 27. One was in Judah and one in Asher.

It appears in the text that the captivity of Samson was to the Philistines a proof that their god had gained the victory over his God. And in 1 Sam. ix. 7, and v. 2, they are found indulging in the same exultation, confident from the ark having fallen into their hands, that Dagon was superior to Jehovah. In like manner the Assyrians, 1 Kings xx. 28, fancy that they have been defeated because they had fought with the Israelites in the hill country, seeing that the God of Israel was a God of the hills, whereas their gods were gods of the valleys. And Pharaoh's haughty defiance of the power of Jehovah clearly implies that he thought him merely the national god of the Hebrews, and greatly inferior to his own gods, and therefore he would not hear his voice, nor let Israel go. Ex. v. 2.

III. We are now introduced to the god of this "solemn feast." Let us consider the house of their worship and its downfall.

From the text we learn that the house in which the Philistine lords were gathered together to offer a great sacrifice unto Dagon, their god, was full of men and women, and that it stood on and was borne up by "two middle pillars." But I think the labour of the learned to prove that this house had but two pillars, all lost. It is not historically true that the ancients made any such structures resting only on two pillars. And so far as the history before us is concerned, there may have been as many pillars to the house of Dagon, as there are in the hall of the thousand pillars of Constantinople, or in the great hall of Karnak, and yet the two céntre pillars being the key to the building, may have so borne it up, that it may be said to have stood on them, and when they were pulled down, the whole edifice fell to the ground.

Sir Christopher Wren's explanation of the structure and fall of this edifice is this. He says: "Conceive a vast roof of cedar beams resting at one end upon the walls, and centering at the other upon one short architrave that united two cedar pillars in the middle. One pillar would not be sufficient to unite the ends of at least one hundred beams that tended to the centre; therefore, I say, there must have been a short architrave resting upon two pillars, upon which all the beams tending to the centre might be supported. Now if Samson, by his miraculous strength, pressing on one or both these pillars, moved it from its basis, the whole roof must of necessity fall."* These remarks from so eminent an architect are commended to the attention of those who deny that the ancients built such structures at all, or if they did, that Samson could have demolished such a one in the manner described in the text. I do not, however, see the necessity of deciding whether the Philistines' building were a temple or a market or a palace. We know that the Egyptians had temples and palaces long before this, and we have found that the Philistines were of Egyptian origin. It is also known that the temples, market places, and palaces were sometimes all united together. The same custom obtained

---

* Hewlett's Bible, quoted by Bush.

subsequently in Greece and Rome. I am aware that it is urged as an objection to the historic verity of the text, that if such a building had been demolished in this way, greater prominence would have been given to such a catastrophe. But the text does not state that all the building fell. It may be that only the wing or protruding portion opposite to the grand entrance, in which the lords and their families were assembled, fell. And besides how do we know that it did not make a profound sensation in all the surrounding country? Where are the annals of the Philistine satrapies that say it did not? It is fairly inferred from the text that it did make a profound impression; for the warrior thousands of Philistia made no resistance to Samson's brethren, who came and took away his body from the ruins, and buried him in the sepulchre of his father Manoah, as a prince and a great man in Israel. At least we are bold to say that there is not a syllable uttered or fairly implied from our record that is inconsistent with the known usages of that age and country. The proof is complete that the ancients constructed vast sacred enclosures. They were generally a kind of amphitheatre or arena, the first tier of which usually came near or quite together on pillars at or opposite to the main opening. The first and lowest tier converged somewhat like the heels of a horse-shoe upon the pillars at the lower side, and rose rapidly behind. Within the walls and under the seats were numerous cloisters or stalls. The seats receded in regular tiers from the open court, which was for the wild beasts and wrestlers or gladiators. Sometimes a portion of the court and of the seats was covered with a flat or gently declining roof. These amphitheatres were the largest structures of the ancients. They were computed to have been large enough to hold from fifty to eighty thousand spectators. The ruins of those of Athens, Nismes, Verona, and Rome, which still exist, prove their magnitude. There is no difficulty then in finding room for the multitude of men and women to witness the sport of the Hebrew captive, nor in explaining how the building or a portion of it, rested on two main key pillars. Nor are we without collateral evidence. Tacitus in his Annals (lib. vi. 62) tells us of an amphitheatre that fell almost in the same way as this house of the Philistines. And Pliny (Hist. Nat. xxxvi. 15) says two theatres at Rome, built by Caius Curio, were large enough to hold all the Roman people, and yet so constructed as to depend upon a single hinge or pivot for support. And Dr. Shaw, in his travels and observations in the Barbary States and Levant, says that he "frequently saw the inhabitants of Algiers diverting themselves upon the Dey's palace; which, like many more of the same quality and denomination, has an advanced cloister over against the gate of the palace, made in the form of a large pent-house, supported only by one or two contiguous pillars in the front, or else in the centre. In such open structures as these, the great officers of state distribute justice, and transact the public affairs of their provinces. Here, likewise, they have their public entertainments, as the lords of the Philistines had in the temple of their god. Supposing, therefore, that in the house of Dagon was a cloistered building of this kind, the pulling down of the front or centre pillars which supported it, would alone be attended with the catastrophe which happened to the Philistines."

Bearing in mind these historic facts—that the ancients used large buildings for the transaction of business, for holding public assemblies, for games, feasts, and religious ceremonies—that such structures were made sometimes round, and sometimes nearly in the shape of a horse-shoe, so that the building was made to rest mainly on two or a few pillars in the foreground or portico, as an arch rests upon a key stone—and then consider the great weight of such an assemblage as was on the roof—and bear in mind, that Samson pulled or pushed one of the pillars with his right hand and the other with his left, and called at the same time upon his God, who strengthened him; and we have no difficulty in believing that at least the portion of the building containing the lords came crashing down with great violence, killing them and crushing those that were below, amongst whom was Samson himself. It is not at all necessary that we should be able to point to a building now in the East exactly like this one. The essential parts of such a structure are to be found, and historically we know such buildings were used by the ancients, and that similar catastrophes have occurred in other places. Everything known of ancient times and of surrounding nations corroborates the truthfulness of the Bible narrative as an authentic history. It must not be overlooked, however, that Samson pulled down the building by the Spirit of the Almighty. Bible histories are not incredible, because they are not impossible, nor under the circumstances are they improbable. The hand of Jehovah was in them. Who then can say they are impossible? The Almighty is never at a loss for agents or means by which to serve his people and fulfil his purposes. Samson, now penitent and forgiven, has his commission restored to him, and in the last acts of his life as in his earlier days, we find him again performing exploits as God's agent.

IV. The superstition of the Philistines misinterpreted the cause of their success against Samson. It was not because their god had prevailed over Samson's God, but because Samson had disobeyed his God. It was owing to his sinning, and not to Dagon's superiority, that he was helpless in their hands. The barbarians of Melita fell into a similar mistake in regard to Paul. It is the nature of all superstitions to make mistakes by arousing false fears, leading to wrong conclusions, and ascribing effects to causes which do not exist. According to their theory and practice on this occasion, when Samson smote them hip and thigh with a great slaughter, and when he slew them "heaps upon heaps with the jaw-bone of an ass," they should have said, "Our god has failed us." When smarting under Samson's blows, they should have said, Where is now our god? Why does he allow our enemy to prevail? But to their praise be it said, we find them more ready to bless than to curse their deity. Whatever may be thought of their idolatry and cruelty, they cannot be charged with ingratitude. They did not forget to ascribe their success to their god. They knew that it was Delilah that had betrayed Samson into their hands, yet as they shouted the praises of Dagon, they said, "Our god hath delivered our enemy into our hands." In their gratitude they are a model to us. Generally men claim all their prosperity as due to themselves, but cast the blame of their miscarriages upon their bad luck, which is their way of accusing Providence. This is both unjust and sinful.

As on a former occasion, so here, their shout was Samson's battle cry. No doubt, their boisterous praise of Dagon was a great mortification to him. He knew they ascribed their success against him to their god, and regarded his fall and disgrace as a proof that Dagon had triumphed over Jehovah. Ah! the dishonour that he felt he had brought upon his religion was his keenest grief. His captivity, blindness, and bodily sufferings were nothing to him in comparison with his agony for having sinned against the living and true God. It was true then, and it is true now, the heathen judge of the Christian's God, not so much by his creed and catechism, as by his conduct and condition in the world. The manners and modes of dealing with the heathen practised by merchants and travellers, form the heathen idea of christianity more directly than any other source of influence.

"And it came to pass when their hearts were merry, that they said, Call for Samson that he may make us sport. And they called for Samson out of the prison-house, and he made them sport: and they set him between the pillars."

Milton says Samson at first refused to attend their feast to make sport before Dagon, but being at length persuaded inwardly that it was an occasion from God, he went. They had power to compel his attendance whether he would or not. He was powerless in their hands. It is not stated here what kind of sport he was to make. The Septuagint and Josephus think their purpose was to insult him, and make him a laughing-stock. According to the Septuagint, "they buffeted him." Josephus says: "He was brought out that they might insult him in their cups." At all events, they would have no other sport but from the great Hebrew. He who had been their terror, must now be their play. Every man, woman, and boy could now laugh at the blind hero, that had once been their most fearful enemy. Scorn is added to misery; insult to injury. No doubt Samson was ready to wish himself deaf as well as blind, that he might not hear their cruel jests and horrid blasphemies. Whether Samson amused them first with some attempts at extraordinary strength, as he was made the butt of their jests or not, he did at last make sport for them with a vengeance. In the East it was common at their feasts to have athletic sports.

But now that the heathen have triumphed, will not God arise? Now that Samson has repented, as did Peter with many bitter tears, and is forgiven—and his hair has grown, and he is again in covenant with his God, how shall his enemies escape? For if judgment begin in God's own house and upon his own chosen servants, what shall be the end of the ungodly, who obey not his voice? Surely it is the hour of long pent up and terrible vengeance. May not Samson now vindicate the superiority of Jehovah over the false Philistine god? Yes; the whole scene is now changed. The contest is no longer between the Hebrew judge and the Philistine lords, but between Dagon and Jehovah. The battle is now to rage on Mount Olympus, and Troy is to be lost or won in heaven, and not on the dusty plains below. From Hebrews xi. it is clear that Samson's prayer was the prayer of sincere faith. It was through faith he prevailed. If he had not been truly penitent, and had not been accepted of God, his last prayer could not have been successful. His struggle of mind must have been great. But out of despair he gathered hope, as his enemies increased in their boisterous blasphemy. The case seemed a desperate one. The temple is full of men and women, making themselves merry at his expense, and in blaspheming the living God. He begins again to feel the Spirit of God stirring him as in years long since past. He remembers that the great commission from heaven announced for him before he was born, was to begin to deliver Israel from the Philistines. He asks himself, May it not be that now I shall be able to vindicate the superiority of God Almighty over this wretched idol, whom his enemies are worshipping? May it not be that for this hour I have been spared, and that now I may most wonderfully redeem my great commission? "And he called upon the Lord, and said, O Lord God, remember me, I pray thee, and strengthen me, I pray thee, only this once, O God. And he took hold of the two middle pillars upon which the house stood and on which it was borne up, of the one with his right hand, and of the other with his left, and said, Let me die with the Philistines."

Solemnly re-dedicating himself to God, consecrating his life as a patriot and a martyr, if God would now be pleased to accept it, as the last, best, and only offering he had to make—praying this once more to be heard, and that he might die with the Philistines, fulfilling in his last act and dying moment the terrible mission for which he had been raised up—as he prayed he bowed himself with all his might, and the house fell upon the lords and upon all the people that were therein. "So the dead which he slew at his death were more than they which he slew in his life." Neither Leonidas nor Lord Nelson had a death so terribly sublime. His was not the suicide's death, but that of a martyr who consecrates himself to death, if such is God's will, in the performance of duty or the maintenance of truth. The result proves that God did graciously condescend to hear his prayer, and to accept his consecration. For without direct supernatural power he could not have thus prevailed over his enemies.

V. It has been objected that Samson's last prayer is not the prayer of a dying christian—that it breathes the spirit of revenge, which is wholly unbecoming a pious man at any time, and much less so in his dying moments. To this we reply:

1. However comforting it may be to a dying man himself and to his surrounding friends to utter nothing but pious words, ecstatic hopes, and fervent supplications—however desirable it may be to die in the full assurance of heaven, almost in sight of the celestial city, as Stephen did—still such experiences and dying deliverances are not required to prove our acceptance with God. A man may be a godly man, and die without such ecstatic joys. The operations of the divine Spirit are manifold. Our experience and utterances of inward life are moulded very much by our temperaments and style of education. Holiness is essential to the enjoyment

of God. And holiness is a habitude, rather than a spasm or temporary emotion; and ordinarily this spiritual habitude is the growth of a life of prayer and godliness under the culture of the Divine Spirit. The life and faith, and not the feelings of a man in his dying moments, are to be taken as exponents of his state in the sight of God.

2. Samson was educated out of the law of the Lord, which required "an eye for an eye, and a tooth for a tooth." Retaliation was his catechism. I do not now consider why such was the law of Moses. The fact is certain. But it is equally certain that our Lord alludes to this very law of Moses, and changes it, saying, It shall no longer be "an eye for an eye;" but I say unto you, Requite not evil with evil; pray for your enemies; forgive them; do good to them that despitefully use you, that you may become the children of your Father which is in heaven. Samson had not then before him, as we have, the example of the meek and suffering God-man. He had not his history in the garden, and in Pilate's hall, and on the cross. He had not heard the prayer, nor any such an one: "Father, forgive them, for they know not what they do." It is not fair, therefore, for us to pronounce on the prayer of the penitent and dying judge from our stand-point of gospel light, but according to the light of Moses's dispensation. We should not expect him to die as Paul did. His mission and character belong wholly to a different dispensation.

3. We must remember that Samson's prayer was in keeping with his divine commission. As a soldier, he dies in the heat of the battle with his armour on. If it was right for him to bear his commission to destroy the Philistines for the vindication of God, and the deliverance of Israel from their oppressors, then his death was in the way of duty. He was sent to execute divine judgments on the oppressors of God's people. He did not, therefore, throw his life

away. He did not lay rash hands upon himself. He did not know what the final result would be, but, as every other soldier who goes into battle for his country and for the truth of God, he puts his life in jeopardy. He takes it in his hands, ready at any moment to offer it up as a sacrifice. As his hair had grown, his experience of divine grace had increased; until now, when God's enemies were at the very highest point of exultation and defiance, the Spirit of the Lord moved him once more—first, to say, "O Lord God, remember me, I pray thee; only this once, O God," and then moved him to lean against the pillars and take hold of them, and at the same time stirred him up to further prayer, saying, If such is now the divine will, in fulfilling my commission, let me even die with the Philistines And the Lord heard his prayer, accepted the offering of his body and soul, and in his death he slew more than in all his life.

> "——Samson hath quit himself
> Like Samson, and heroicly hath finished
> A life heroic."

## CHAPTER XVII.

### THE EPILOGUE AND ITS TEACHINGS.

——" Like a visitant
From the other world, he comes as if to haunt
Thy guilty soul with dreams of lost delight,
Long lost to all but memory's aching sight;—
———As when the spirit of our youth
Returns in sleep, sparkling with all the truth
And innocence once ours, and leads us back
In mournful mockery, o'er the shining track
Of our young life, and points out every ray
Of hope and peace we've lost upon the way."
*Lalla Rookh.*

THE late venerable Dr. Miller of Princeton, N. J., who was one of the most perfect and well balanced men as a scholar, theologian, and christian gentleman, this country has ever produced, used to say, that if a student had sense enough to bear it, it was an advantage to put him to studying a text book that required some corrections; for the detection of the errors and their correction helped amazingly to keep up the attention, and draw out his own resources. There is certainly such a thing as being so straight as to lean over. There may be so much straining of rules as to destroy all the benefits of discipline. Children were made to play as well as study, to laugh heartily as well as to think seriously. The bow always bent is sometimes converted into a strait jacket. To laugh well is medicine for the body and the mind, and to be able to wonder well is a great blessing. One of the old fathers, (and may his shadow never be less,) Clemens Alexandrinus, says: "The beginning of truth is to wonder, for this proceeds from conscious ignorance." The old Stagyrite had taught almost the same thing before the Alexandrine was born, when he said, It is by wondering men begin to love philosophy and to grow wise. (Aristotle. Metaph. 1, 2.) It is true, however, that there is a kind of foolish wonder, that does not promise much good—but even that is not so hopeless as ignorance so profound as to be unconscious of its own existence. It were better men should be astrologers than that they should be so stupid as not to know that there are any stars over their heads. I should rather undertake to teach those that are stone-blind, than those who are so stupid and indolent, that they will not open their eyes; for the stone-blind feel and acknowledge their blindness, and may learn to read without eyes; whereas the others are so self-sufficient and content with their blindness that they either deny that they are blind at all, or declare it best to be blind. Nothing is so hopeless as ignorance too complete to wonder; for then there are no errors that may lead to a knowledge of truth. If the beginning of wisdom is to fear God and know ourselves, then may we say that the faculty to wonder is a shadow of something beautiful and good to come. I do not belong to the school that would blot out from our juvenile literature the seven wise men of Gotham, Blue Beard, Jack the Giant Killer, Robinson Crusoe, the Arabian Nights, and fairy tales in general. By no means. In judicious hands this species of literature is invaluable for training and purifying the youthful mind. It were far better to excite the love of the marvellous, and even of the terribly sublime than of the gross and sensual. After the nursery period well employed, some five or six authors are quite enough to train the intellect and heart. Who needs to know more than he can learn from the Bible, Homer, Dante, Shakspeare, Bacon, and Milton, and a few standard historians?

The sacred story of Israel's giant judge is a wonderful one, but it is as true as marvellous. It is a simple, earnest, straight forward narrative of a man—a real man, and of what he did, and of what befel him in just such a world as we live in, and among men, women, and children exactly such as we are. We believe the Bible Samson is the original of all the stories of Hercules that fill so many pages of heathen literature. And by exciting attention to his life, we hope, on the love of the wonderful, to plant a lever that shall turn the whole heart to truth. Joseph, Daniel, Nehemiah, and various other Bible heroes are more to our liking; but, if "there is," as the bard of Avon says, "a history in all men's lives," I fancy Samson's is not an exception, and as his biography has been given to us by the Holy Spirit, it is our duty to remove objections to it, and see what it teaches us. As already intimated, Samson's acts are more for our wonder than for our imitation; nevertheless important principles are unfolded in his history. Much as Milton's Samson Agonistes is to be admired as a whole, it seems to us, he wholly fails to appreciate his character. The dying speech which he puts into his mouth as he pulls down the temple is not true to the text, nor worthy of the occasion. It falls far below our idea of Samson in that awful moment. His enemies were in force around him, mocking him and his God. He knew that it was their custom on such occasions, after they had satisfied themselves with feastings and sport, to sacrifice their chief prisoner to their gods. In this great extremity, therefore, he betook himself to prayer for grace to triumph in a martyr's death, if the Lord would be pleased to grant him such an honour. Having eyes now to see Him who is invisible, he said: "O Lord God, I pray thee think upon me; O Lord God, I beseech thee strengthen me at this time only. For thy great name's sake—for thy glory among the heathen, help me, O Lord, help me this one time." It was zeal for the divine glory, and to retrieve the honour of the God of his fathers, that had been tarnished by his fall, that made him so anxious now to die in such a way as to fulfil in his death, more fully than he had done in his life, the mission for which he had been raised up. As he knew he was now about to die, he seized this as the last opportunity to deliver Israel, and show that Jehovah and not Dagon was the true and living God. In his death scene, therefore, we see fast by his side again the presence of the Angel—

> "Who from his father's field
> Rode up in flames
> From off the altar, where an offering burned,
> As in a fiery column charioting."

When dying we see him filled again with—

> "That Spirit that first rushed upon him in the camp of Dan."

The lordly city of Gaza speaks then to us historically, from a period beyond which the memory of man runneth not. It was once the treasure-house of a Persian conqueror, as indeed its name is supposed to signify. But how its name came to be prophetic of its treasures, we know not. True, Philistine Sheikhs, Arabian Emirs, Assyrian, Persian, Egyptian, Greek, and Roman conquerors and kings have battled for its gates. Saladin the magnificent, and Richard the lion-heart, and Napoleon the great took some of life's stern lessons under the skies that still look down on Gaza. Ancient Gaza is all in ruins—shapeless, nameless ruins—capitals, architraves, columns, cornices, and marble floors, the cedar, fir, and acacia, alabaster, and granite, that once echoed to the shouts of the worshippers of the great fish-god, though now unlettered, still utter forth a loud and distinctly articulate voice. Its stores of wine and oil, and treasures of jewels and costly spices are no more; but Gaza still has for us treasures more valuable—lessons of instruction and warning—not only to those who are driving through life with a Jehu speed in fulfilling the lusts of the eye and the pride of the mind; but for all, old and young, and of every class. The marvellous career of the giant judge, and his tragical end is a lesson for our every-day life.

1. Samson's life illustrates God's long-suffering and mercy. When evil doers are allowed for a time to go on in prosperity, they should not presume, for there is a righteous God, that judgeth in the earth; and when his judgments fall on the guilty, he will cut short his awful work in terrible righteousness. But mercy is remembered amidst deserved wrath. The penitent is not therefore to despair, for God is merciful as well as just. Samson may fall into the hands of the Philistines; even the ark of God may be in the camp of the uncircumcised, and be brought into the temple of their great Dagon; but Jehovah is still supreme over all the gods. His arm is still omnipotent. There is indeed no god but God. The idols of the heathen are all vanity and lies. The ruins of the house of the Philistine lords, and the dismembered image of Dagon in his own temple before Jehovah's ark, are directly in proof, that their god is not as our God, even our enemies themselves being judges.

2. Jehovah is the only sovereign. His government is supreme over all tribes and nations. The history of the Canaanites, Philistines, and Hebrews proves that it is Jehovah's pleasure to take cognizance of all his creatures on

earth—to observe and rule over them as families, peoples, and individuals. As all the spokes of a wheel turn 'round when the wheel revolves, so a general providence necessarily implies a particular oversight of all the universe. How else could there have been any prophecy, or fulfilment of promises? In the prophecies fulfilled, and in those yet to be accomplished, we find an individual and a national application. The prophecies referred sometimes in part to the personal history of the individual, but generally or chiefly to his posterity. This is true of Abraham, Ishmael, Esau, and Jacob. Hence the distinctness with which the line of their descendants was preserved. It were a great gain for the politics and economics of communities and nations if the providence of God were more distinctly recognized. Every chapter of our national history is replete with proofs of God's presence. His hand has written all our history.

3. Again it appears that God governs the world upon eternal principles—and not from fancy or passion. These principles are still in actual operation. *A priori*, we should argue that such must be the divine government of the universe, and historically we find it pre-eminently so. The Creator is as really supreme over modern nations, as over ancient nations. Jehovah was as truly the God of Washington as of Moses, only Moses was his lieutenant in an age of miracles. It is as true now as it was then, that sin defiles a land, and that God blesses obedience and punishes disobedience to his laws. Divine laws in morals are as immutable as in physics. God is just as supreme in the streets of the city as in the pathways of the planets. His ear is as open to prayer now, as it ever was in Solomon's temple. And happiness everywhere, in heaven and earth, is nothing but a full hearted, cheerful harmony with the will of God. In keeping his commandments, there is great reward.

4. When patience has done its perfect work—when the hour of retribution has fully come, then there is no escape from the Almighty. The universe itself in ruins and in heaps upon heaps upon the guilty could not hide them from the all-seeing eye, nor prevent Him from bringing them to judgment. The old world, the Egyptians, the cities of the plain, and the history of the chosen people, as well as of the Philistines and Canaanites, prove this.

5. But Samson's life illustrates divine laws in their application as well as in theory. In solving the riddle of his character we have truth objective and subjective. The glimpses we get of his spiritual life are sad enough. His weakness and inconsistencies are so mortifying as to be almost incredible. His infatuation for Philistine women rendered him apparently blind to their heathenism and their enmity towards Israel. Philistine maids frequently vanquished the champion that was to deliver Israel out of the hands of their oppressive countrymen. An old writer very nearly expresses the facts of this history, when he says, it was not so much Samson that overcame the Philistine men, as Philistine women that conquered Samson.

6. Sin is an awfully steep precipice, and as slippery as steep. I know we are ready to cry out at Samson's stupidity, and Delilah's impudent treachery. And truly never was a man so overcome by flagons of wine, as this Nazarite was by his love for Delilah. We are almost ready to think Samson must have been void of common sense, when, after she had betrayed him three times, he should listen to her fourth proposal, and actually yield. And yet are there none of you, that have yielded to temptation not only three times, and then a fourth time, but ten times ten? Is not every transgressor against God's laws as stupid as our infatuated judge? Sinful pleasures lodged and entertained in our bosoms are as dangerous and as treacherous as Deli-

lah. In our better moments we know they aim at nothing less than our destruction. We know the wages of sin is death, and yet we yield! Every one that yields to the intoxicating cup, to the strange woman's smiles, or to the demon of fraud or of gambling, is like Samson sleeping in Delilah's lap, to wake up bereft of strength and peace of mind. Thrice the armed Philistines came out of their hiding-place to bind him, and yet he yields to the fourth temptation. Oh, what madness! Fly at once. Resist the devil and he will flee from you. But if you parley with him, he will bind you fast in his chains.

All sins hang together like links in a chain. Delilah was a heathen. She had not the fear of God before her eyes, and as she wanted virtue, it is not strange that she was perfidious. And so like india-rubber is conscience now-a-days, that, if it is used at all, it is easily stretched, and though hard to be washed clean, it is nevertheless often turned. So naturally and lovingly do sinful ways run together and follow each other, that men do often educate their conscience to call good evil, and evil good: and

> "Compound for sins they are inclined to,
> By damning those they have no mind to."

If in straining at a gnat, they do not swallow a camel the first time, they will soon be able, from repeated trials, to swallow the whole caravan, gnats, and all. The liar is not satisfied till he steals; and the thief soon kills. The drunkard is as lewd as he is full of wine, and she that traffics with her personal charms is as false as she is vile. And he that dwells with a concubine, to avoid the manly responsibilities of a lawful family, finds in the end that instead of having a jewel around his neck, he has bound himself, soul and body, to a burning millstone, that is dragging him hissing down to the pit. A person given up to one sin is sold to iniquity. By yielding to one sin, a greater susceptibility is created for others, and in the same proportion he is shorn of strength to resist temptation and to maintain his hold on virtue. He that does not make it a matter of conscience to abide by right principles in everything and everywhere, is not to be trusted in anything.

7. We see that an ill-balanced character is a sadly defective one. If Samson had been as prudent as he was strong, as pious as he was patriotic, what a splendid hero he would have been! But symmetry of character is also sadly wanting in modern times. Some are remarkable for their zeal, who make their public concern for the conversion of men cover their want of attention to their own families. But can a man be called of God to one duty at the expense of another—and in this case of a prior and paramount one? Others are remarkable for their denominational or church zeal, but their daily walk is so irregular, that even when they are not absolutely guilty of moral delinquencies in the sight of the law, their advocacy of religion is not a recommendation. Others are text-quoting defenders of the Bible, but the light that is in them is smothered. The word of God dwells in them, but is not fruitful. They are cold as icicles. Another takes the Bible for his directory. He loves its truth, and he has some experimental knowledge of divine grace in his heart; but he is so ill-tempered, so peevish, so irritable, that the symmetry of his character is destroyed. Men admit his sincerity of purpose, but wonder that so good a man should be so weak as to allow himself to be carried away with passion. Oh, how much would the church gain if all its members were complete in Christ!

8. In Samson's life we see that constitutional sins are peculiarly dangerous. It is true God employs men as his agents, who are not perfect. Even great men are not with-

out errors. Believers on earth are not saints glorified. In the course of this work it has been intimated several times that we have only a skeleton history of the giant judge. Of long periods we have no memoir at all, and of great achievements we have but a simple record of the fact. His faults are detailed. His good deeds not so fully chronicled. If we may say so without irreverence, our narrative does not seem to take pleasure in his exploits, but simply to set forth how divine sovereignty overruled them. His attachment to the Timnite, his fall at Gaza, and his blind affection for Delilah, and his conflicts with the Philistines are recorded so far as seemed to be necessary to furnish us with the proof that the promise to his parents was faithfully kept, and no more. It seems almost as if infinite wisdom here illustrated how sorry an agent might perform mighty deeds, and how sovereign grace could at last reign where sin had abounded.

9. Samson's life very properly leads us to the purity, sacredness, and stability of the marriage relation. The family is the foundation stone for national well-being. We must at any price, at any and every sacrifice, preserve our christian homes, as the fountains of principle and piety And never was there an age nor a people with whom so much depended upon the maintenance of sound principles and of true religion in the family as with us. If we yield here, all is lost. Our public institutions will be as the new cords on Samson's arms, mere cinders, if the principles of high morality and true religion are not taught in our homes. Thorough training and instruction must be given to the children of this Republic. And this work must be begun early at home, and continued long at home, and the school must never supersede the home. We have found Manoah's solicitude about the bringing up of his angel-announced son natural and proper. It is a great mistake to consider the

education of a child an individual blessing rather than a general one—personal, rather than social. The advantages of education are indeed personal, and just in so far as they are a blessing to the individual members of society, in the same degree they are a blessing to society itself. The Bible teaches us that no one has a right to segregate himself from his fellow-men, with Cain-like indifference for their well-being. But an educated mind has extensive relations with the world. It is then contrary to the first and highest claims of humanity that it should refuse to shed its benign influences upon society. Nay, it is impossible to escape such a responsibility. Intellect can no more exist without responsibility, than matter without gravitation. Responsibility is as inseparable from our individual existence as our personal identity. Escape from it is as impossible as annihilation. We must, then, meet it as men, and justify the claims of God and man upon us, or turn traitors to the society of the universe and its ineffable Creator. In the measure, therefore, that we are blessed with talents, faculties, and attainments, are our responsibilities increased. "Where much is given, much is required. He that knows his Lord's will, and does it not, shall be beaten with many stripes." As the glory of a State is but the aggregated glory of its several citizens, so whatever contributes to the mental enjoyment, social worth, productive industry, commercial reputation for integrity, and to the moral elevation of the individual members of the State, must be regarded as contributing also to its welfare and glory. The received maxim, then, that it is easier and cheaper to prevent crime, than to vindicate the laws and reform the transgressor, should be universally put into practice. The vices of ignorance and depravity cost the State more than school-houses and teachers. The public safety under a free government requires that all the youth be instructed in knowledge and morality. And in attaining such blessings the greatest good of individuals is identical with that of the community. For a number of years there has been no want of energy on the part of the press of Great Britain and this country in advocating the enlightenment of the people in order to the enjoyment of free institutions. We are almost wearied with references to Greece and Rome, and the attempts at Republics in past ages by people not capable of preserving freedom, nor indeed able to comprehend what it is. The Ionian islands are a remarkable instance, however, that is not so often referred to. Their history is a striking illustration of the hopelessness of a people undertaking to govern themselves without the requisite intelligence, morality, and religion. They have played very nearly the same game for many years. "Three times, at very wide intervals, has Corfu (the ancient Corcyra) found it necessary to abnegate, more or less completely, a political independence of which it was incapable, and to place itself under the sovereignty or protection of the power which in each of those respective ages was mistress of the seas."* At one time Corcyra was obliged to seek abroad refuge from her own selfish policy and her own internal factions by throwing herself into the arms of Athens. At another time she was compelled to seek protection against herself under the banner of Venice. And then again from an abortive attempt to form a Republic, the Ionians threw themselves at the feet of Russia, then of France, and finally passed under the protectorate of Great Britain. In 1802 they sent M. Naranzi as envoy to Alexander, Emperor of Russia, begging that with an "imposing armed force," he would save them from the cruel sufferings of their attempts at self-government. They directed their envoy to say to the Czar: "That the inhabitants of the seven islands, who

* London Quarterly Review, October, 1852, p. 168.

had attempted to establish a republican form of government, are neither born free, nor are they instructed in any art of government, nor are they possessed of moderation so as to live peaceably under any government formed by their own countrymen." This was certainly very remarkable language for a people having intelligence enough to struggle to be free, and yet not able to govern themselves. But all history is a demonstration of its correctness. Italy and France, Central and South America are monuments proving to all the world that sanctified intelligence among the people alone can save them from the cruelties of self government. Mere knowledge is not enough. There must be constitutional laws, and right principles must be deeply implanted in the bosoms of those that would be free. Men can not govern themselves unless they abide immutably by the laws and constitution that guarantee their freedom. The great English historian* has, in his usually happy way, described the very danger we so seriously apprehend. "I remember," says he, "that Adam Smith and Gibbon had told us that there would never again be a destruction of civilization by barbarians. The flood, they said, would no more return to cover the earth; and they seemed to reason justly, for they compared the immense strength of the civilized part of the world with the weakness of that part which remained savage, and asked from whence were to come those Huns, and from whence were to come those Vandals, who were again to destroy civilization? Alas! it did not occur to them that civilization itself might engender the barbarians who should destroy it. It did not occur to them that in the very heart of great capitals, in the very neighbourhood of splendid palaces, and churches, and theatres, and libraries, and museums, vice and ignorance and misery

* Macaulay's speech at Edinburgh.

might produce a race of Huns fiercer than those who marched under Attila, and Vandals more bent on destruction than those who followed Genseric."

10. Samson is a pictorial of a mother's anxiety and influence. We have no powers of analysis sufficient to disintegrate the virtue, and freedom, and prosperity of modern Christendom, so as to show the proportion and amount of its well-doing and well-being that is distinctly to be traced to the influence of christian mothers; but it is paramount to all other sources of power. For example, who can measure the forming energy of Washington upon the destinies of the American people and of the world? And yet in the chronicles of the invisible world the character of that great patriot was formed by the training of his mother. And upon examination, we find his mother's favourite author to have been the great christian judge, the English Sir Matthew Hale. The identical copy she used is still cherished as an heir-loom, in the family. Now in the "Contemplations" of Sir Matthew Hale we have an essay on "The Good Steward," and a series of "Meditations" on the Lord's Prayer. And in those works of the learned and pious judge, we find the germs of Washington's great character. These works were his mother's manual when she was training him for the high destinies for which a supreme providence was preparing him. Here we have the very principles taught, and the very precepts inculcated, that were fitted to produce the traits characteristic of the American patriot. Moderation, self-control, sobriety, integrity, and a well-balanced judgment, and an habitual recognition of God's will and dependence on an overruling providence, have great prominence in the Briton's pages. And these are the very elements of Washington's character. More than one hundred times we find him in his letters, speaking of his dependence on God's providence. And

throughout his life, we have "the composure of the Areopagus carried into the struggles of Thermopylæ." The beauty and the glory of his character is its combination of integrity, moral goodness, heroic courage, with judicial sagacity and serenity amid all the fierce conflicts of a great and successful Revolution. What mother is there, then, who is not willing to forego some, or all the pleasures of fashion, and spend her strength in teaching, and toiling, and praying for her child, seeing that it is given to her by the Great Father of all spirits, more than to any other, to unseal the fountain of its being and form the channel in which it is to flow for ever? The mother's example and lessons are the passages of experimental divinity and social philosophy that are never forgotten. By them we both live and die. The tribute which one of our Chief Magistrates, John Quincy Adams, paid to his mother, expresses what almost every one feels to be true. "It is due," said he, "to gratitude and nature, that I should acknowledge and avow that, such as I have been, whatever it was, such as I am, whatever it is, and such as I hope to be in all futurity, must be ascribed, under providence, to the precepts, prayers, and example of my mother."

Finally. We beseech you, young men, because you are strong, remember your responsibility for your influence upon society. You are invested with an immortality that you cannot lay aside. When you die and leave the world into which you have been born, your influence will walk the earth and represent you where you personally will be known no more. Aim then by God's help to be a fountain of good influences and not of evil. In Samson you have a solemn warning against the wiles of the strange woman, of whom Solomon has said: "I find more bitter than death the woman whose heart is snares and nets, and her hands are bands;

whoso pleaseth God shall escape from her; but the sinner shall be taken by her."

Forget not your dedication to God, nor disappoint the just expectations of your friends. Ponder well what your country expects of you. Remember your patrimony and your age. Fill your minds with objects illustrious as your antecedents are hopeful. You are surrounded by living voices calling you to maintain the principles and faith of sires passed into glory. Put on the whole armour of light, and by self-control, and by high principles, and by an incorruptible love for truth and for your country, rebuke whatever billows may arise to threaten the ark of your fathers, and make them roll at your feet soft as the swelling of a summer's sea. Serve well your generation according to the will of God, and then when you are laid to rest, though it be far from the home of your youth, and in dust that knoweth not the bones of your fathers, still you will rest in peace, and the everlasting God will be your eternal portion. Whatever good you do in the world will live and come home with its harvest of glory at the judgment day; and whatever evil you do, if not repented of and forgiven, will go on increasing its guilt until it is garnered on your heart amid the awful realities of eternity. They that turn many to righteousness shall shine as the stars of the firmament for ever and ever; and they that have turned many to evil shall burn as pyramids of fire, embosoming, like so many unquenchable molochs, the souls of those they have seduced from truth and innocence, and dragged down to ruin; and the curses of all good men, and of all the holy angels, and of God Almighty, shall fall upon them for ever and ever.

"AND THOU, MY SON, KNOW THOU THE GOD OF THY FATHER, AND SERVE HIM WITH A PERFECT HEART AND

WITH A WILLING MIND: FOR THE LORD SEARCHETH ALL HEARTS, AND UNDERSTANDETH ALL THE IMAGINATIONS OF THE THOUGHTS: IF THOU SEEK HIM, HE WILL BE FOUND OF THEE: IF THOU FORSAKE HIM, HE WILL CAST THEE OFF FOR EVER."

THE END.

www.ingramcontent.com/pod-product-compliance
Lightning Source LLC
LaVergne TN
LVHW012327100826
845148LV00017B/391
*9781425521189*